# Rites of Passage

## THEMES IN RELIGIOUS STUDIES SERIES

Series Editors: Jean Holm, with John Bowker

**Other titles**

*Worship*
*Making Moral Decisions*
*Myth and History*
*Attitudes to Nature*
*Picturing God*
*Human Nature and Destiny*
*Sacred Writings*
*Women in Religion*
*Sacred Place*

# Rites of Passage

*Edited by*

Jean Holm

with John Bowker

PINTER
PUBLISHERS
LONDON, NEW YORK

Distributed in the United States and Canada by St. Martin's Press

**Pinter Publishers Ltd.**
25 Floral Street, London WC2E 9DS, United Kingdom

First published in 1994



Distributed exclusively in the USA and Canada by St. Martin's Press, Inc., Room 400, 175 Fifth Avenue, New York, NY 10010, USA

**British Library Cataloguing in Publication Data**

A CIP catalogue record for this book is available from the British Library

ISBN 1 85567 102 6 (hb)
ISBN 1 85567 103 4 (pb)

**Library of Congress Cataloging in Publication Data**

Rites of passage / edited by Jean Holm, with John Bowker.
p. cm. – (Themes in religious studies series)
Includes bibliographical references and index.
ISBN 1–85567–102–6 (hb). – ISBN 1–85567–103–4 (pb).
1. Rites and ceremonies. 2. Life cycle, Human–Religious aspects.
3. Religions. I. Holm, Jean, 1922– . II. Bowker, John Westerdale. III. Series.
BL600.R573 1994
291.3'8–dc20 94–13744
CIP

Typeset by Mayhew Typesetting, Rhayader, Powys
Printed and bound in Great Britain by Biddles Ltd., Guildford and King's Lynn

# Contents

# Series Preface

The person who knows only one religion does not know any religion. This rather startling claim was made in 1873, by Friedrich Max Müller, in his book, *Introduction to the Science of Religion*. He was applying to religion a saying of the poet Goethe: 'He who knows one language, knows none.'

In many ways this series illustrates Max Müller's claim. The diversity among the religious traditions represented in each of the volumes shows how mistaken are those people who assume that the pattern of belief and practice in their own religion is reflected equally in other religions. It is, of course, possible to do a cross-cultural study of the ways in which religions tackle particular issues, such as those which form the titles of the ten books in this series, but it soon becomes obvious that something which is central in one religion may be much less important in another. To take just three examples: the contrast between Islam's and Sikhism's attitudes to pilgrimage, in *Sacred Place*; the whole spectrum of positions on the authority of scriptures illustrated in *Sacred Writings*; and the problem which the titles, *Picturing God* and *Worship*, created for the contributor on Buddhism.

The series offers an introduction to the ways in which the themes are approached within eight religious traditions. Some of the themes relate particularly to the faith and practice of individuals and religious communities (*Picturing God, Worship, Rites of Passage, Sacred Writings, Myth and History, Sacred Place*); others have much wider implications, for society in general as well as for the religious communities themselves (*Attitudes to Nature, Making Moral Decisions, Human Nature and Destiny, Women in Religion*). This distinction, however, is not clear-cut. For instance, the 'sacred places' of Ayodhya and Jerusalem have figured in situations of national and international conflict, and some countries have passed laws regulating, or even banning, religious worship.

Stereotypes of the beliefs and practices of religions are so widespread that a real effort, of both study and imagination, is needed in order to discover what a religion looks – and feels – like to its adherents. We have to bracket out, temporarily, our own beliefs and presuppositions, and 'listen in' to a religion's account of what *it* regards as significant. This is not a straightforward task, and readers of the books in this series will encounter a number of the issues that characterise the study of religions, and that have to be taken into account in any serious attempt to get behind a factual description of a religion to an understanding of the real meaning of the words and actions for its adherents.

First, the problem of language. Islam's insistence that the Arabic of the Qur'ān cannot be 'translated' reflects the impossibility of finding in another language an exact equivalent of many of the most important terms in a religion. The very word, Islam, means something much more positive to a Muslim than is suggested in English by 'submission'. Similarly, it can be misleading to use 'incarnation' for *avatāra* in Hinduism, or 'suffering' for *dukkha* in Buddhism, or 'law' for Torah in Judaism, or 'gods' for *kami* in Shinto, or 'heaven' for *T'ien* in Taoism, or 'name' for *Nām* in Sikhism.

Next, the problem of defining – drawing a line round – a religion. Religions do not exist in a vacuum; they are influenced by the social and cultural context in which they are set. This can affect what they strenuously reject as well as what they may absorb into their pattern of belief and practice. And such influence is continuous, from a religion's origins (even though we may have no records from that period), through significant historical developments (which sometimes lead to the rise of new movements or sects), to its contemporary situation, especially when a religion is transplanted into a different region. For example, anyone who has studied Hinduism in India will be quite unprepared for the form of Hinduism they will meet in the island of Bali.

Even speaking of a 'religion' may be problematic. The term, 'Hinduism', for example, was invented by western scholars, and would not be recognised or understood by most 'Hindus'. A different example is provided by the religious situation in Japan, and the consequent debate among scholars as to whether they should speak of Japanese 'religion' or Japanese 'religions'.

Finally, it can be misleading to encounter only one aspect of a religion's teaching. The themes in this series are part of a whole interrelated network of beliefs and practices within each religious tradition, and need to be seen in this wider context. The reading lists at the end of each chapter point readers to general studies of the religions as well as to books which are helpful for further reading on the themes themselves.

*Jean Holm*
*November 1993*

# List of Contributors

**Jean Holm** (*EDITOR*) was formerly Principal Lecturer in Religious Studies at Homerton College, Cambridge, teaching mainly Judaism and Hinduism. Her interests include relationships between religions; the relationship of culture to religion; and the way in which children are nurtured within a different cultural context. Her publications include *Teaching Religion in School* (Oxford University Press, 1975), *The Study of Religions* (Sheldon, 1977), *Growing up in Judaism* (Longman, 1990), *Growing up in Christianity*, with Romie Ridley (Longman, 1990) and *A Keyguide to Sources of Information on World Religions* (Mansell, 1991). She has edited three previous series: *Issues in Religious Studies*, with Peter Baelz (Sheldon), *Anselm Books*, with Peter Baelz (Lutterworth) and *Growing up in a Religion* (Longman).

**John Bowker** (*EDITOR*) was Professor of Religious Studies in Lancaster University, before returning to Cambridge to become Dean and Fellow of Trinity College. He is at present Professor of Divinity at Gresham College in London, and Adjunct Professor at the University of Pennsylvania and at the State University of North Carolina. He is particularly interested in anthropological and sociological approaches to the study of religions. He has done a number of programmes for the BBC, including the *Worlds of Faith* series, and a series on Islam and Hinduism for the World Service. He is the author of many books in the field of Religious Studies, including *The Meanings of Death* (Cambridge University Press, 1991), which was awarded the biennial Harper Collins religious book prize in 1993, in the academic section.

**Douglas Davies** is Professor of Religious Studies in the Department of Theology at the University of Nottingham, where he specialises in teaching the social anthropology of religion. He trained both in theology and social anthropology and his research continues to relate to both disciplines. His interest in theoretical and historical aspects of religious studies is represented in a major study of the sociology of knowledge and religion, published as *Meaning and Salvation in Religious Studies* (Brill, 1984), and in a historical volume *Frank Byron Jevons 1858–1936, An Evolutionary Realist* (Edwin Mellen Press, 1991). Professor Davies is also very much concerned with practical aspects of religious behaviour and is a leading British scholar of Mormonism and, in addition to various articles, is author of *Mormon Spirituality* (Nottingham and Utah University Press, 1987). He was joint Director of the Rural Church Project, involving one of the largest sociological studies of religion in Britain published as *Church and Religion in Rural Britain* (with C. Watkins and M. Winter, T. & T. Clark, 1991). As Director of the Cremation Research Project he is conducting basic work on Cremation in Britain and Europe and has already produced some results in *Cremation Today and Tomorrow* (Grove Books, 1990).

**Christopher Lamb**, Lecturer in Indian Religions in the School of Philosophy and Religious Studies, Middlesex University, is also Head of the newly founded Centre for Inter-Faith Dialogue. His research is in the Tibetan religious biography, the *rnam-thar*, which he is pursuing at the School of Oriental and African Studies (SOAS), University of London. At present he is engaged in introducing the new computer technology into the teaching of traditional Humanities subjects. He has recently co-operated on a project, 'Animated Graphics in Industry', funded jointly by the Department of Education and Science and industrial partners, to produce, as a means of teaching Buddhist cosmology, a hypermedia version of the Tibetan game of *Rebirth*, invented in the early thirteenth century by the Sa-skya *pandita*, and he has also received external funding for two years to author a hypermedia package on Hindu polytheism. A longer-term project in view is a collaborative venture, *The Cathedral as Text*, which will use the structure of the medieval cathedral as its graphical metaphor, providing a hypertext resource for medieval studies, art history and religious studies.

**Gavin Flood** is Lecturer in Religious Studies at the University of

Wales, Lampeter, where he teaches on courses on Indian Religions and New Religious Movements. His research interests include Śaivism and Hindu Tantra, ritual, and the understandings of the self in Indian religions. He has published articles on Kashmir Śaivism and is author of *Consciousness Embodied: A Study in the Monistic Saivism of Kashmir* (Mellen Press).

**Clinton Bennett** is a Lecturer in Study of Religions at Westminster College, Oxford, and a Baptist Minister. His research interests include Islamic theology and philosophy, historical and contemporary encounter between Muslims and non-Muslims, Islam and anthropology, and religious beliefs as agents of social transformation. Dr Bennett, who edits *Discernment: An Ecumenical Journal of Inter-Religious Encounter*, is the author of *Victorian Images of Islam* (1992), has travelled and worked in the Muslim world, and was a member of the World Council of Churches' (WCC) working party that produced *Issues in Christian–Muslim Relations: Ecumenical Considerations* (1991). He currently serves on the WCC's 'Consultation on the Church and the Jewish People'.

**Alan Unterman** is Minister of the Yeshurun Synagogue, Gatley, Cheshire, and part-time Lecturer in Comparative Religion (Judaism and Hinduism) at the University of Manchester. He studied at the Universities of Birmingham, Oxford and Delhi and at *yeshivot* in London and Jerusalem. He has worked and taught in Israel and Australia. Among his publications are *The Wisdom of the Jewish Mystics*, *Jews: Their Religious Beliefs and Practices*, *Judaism and Art*, 'A Jewish Perspective on the Rushdie Affair' in *The Salman Rushdie Controversy in Interreligious Perspective*, and *A Dictionary of Jewish Lore and Legend.*

**Sewa Singh Kalsi** is Lecturer in Sikh Studies at the University of Leeds, where he specialises in teaching Sikhism and the development of Sikh tradition in Britain. He is author of *The Evolution of a Sikh Community in Britain: Religious and Social Change Among the Sikhs of Leeds and Bradford* (Department of Theology and Religious Studies, University of Leeds, 1992). He has published articles on the development of Sikh tradition in Britain. Dr Kalsi was Senior Lecturer at Bradford and Ilkley Community College where he taught South Asian Studies to undergraduate students for several years. He is actively involved in promoting community relations and multicultural education in Leeds – currently he is Chairman of the Leeds Race Equality Council and member of the Governing Board of Leeds Metropolitan University.

**Xinzhong Yao** is Lecturer in Chinese religion and ethics at the University of Wales, Lampeter. His research interests include philosophy, ethics and religion; he is currently focusing on comparative philosophy and comparative religion. Dr Yao is author of *On Moral Activity* (People's University Press, Beijing, 1990), *Ethics and Social Problems* (City Economic Press, Beijing, 1989), co-author of *Comparative Studies on Human Nature* (Tienjin People's Press, Tienjin, 1988), co-editor of *Applying Ethics* (Jilin People's Press, Changchun, 1994), and main translator of Charles Stevenson's *Ethics and Language* (Social Sciences of China Press, Beijing, 1991). He is a member of the Association of Ethical Studies of China, and Deputy Director of the Institute of Ethics, People's University of China, Beijing.

**Ian Reader** is Senior Lecturer in the Department of Japanese Studies at the University of Stirling, Scotland. He has spent several years in Japan travelling, teaching at Japanese universities and researching into contemporary Japanese religion. His major research interest is in the study of pilgrimage, and he is currently working on a volume on pilgrimage in Japan. Dr Reader is author of *Religion in Contemporary Japan* (Macmillan, 1991), and editor (with Tony Walter) of *Pilgrimage in Popular Culture* (Macmillan, 1992). He has also published numerous articles in journals and collected editions on Buddhism, Japanese religion, pilgrimage and Japanese popular culture, and is a member of the Editorial Advisory Board of the *Japanese Journal of Religious Studies*.

# Introduction: Raising the Issues

*Douglas Davies*

The idea of rites of passage first emerged as a technical term in social anthropology early in the twentieth century. It described the ritual process accompanying the movement of people from one social status to another, as from being a boy to a man or from being a married woman to becoming a mother. As time went on the idea gained popularity outside anthropology so that, for example, in 1980, William Golding could publish a novel with the title *Rites of Passage* and expect it to mean something to the public at large.

## Life and change

Behind the idea of rites of passage lies the fact that the whole of human life is marked by change. Babies are conceived, born, grow, mature, produce offspring and finally die, all as part of the biological facts of life. This has been studied by biologists and anthropologists in theories of ageing and changes in the 'life-course' (Spencer 1990). But this change is not simply a biological process. Because men and women are social as well as biological beings, these changes are not allowed to pass unnoticed. They come to have some value added to them and are interpreted through communal celebration of some sort.

In addition to the biological and social levels of significance, changes in human life have often been interpreted through religious ideas and marked by religious ritual. So, for example, the process of development from birth to death has often been extended into another dimension as the dead are reckoned to become ancestors, or to enter some sort of life after death. The help of supernatural powers is often invoked to give power or protection to those undergoing these changes, as each of the following chapters demonstrates for the great religious traditions of the world.

## Rites of passage

The actual idea of rites of passage emerged as an attempt to interpret the ritual events marking the various social changes experienced by members of society as they progressed through life. Many cultures use their religious beliefs to explain these periods of changing status and to organise the rites in a religious way. As a concept, 'rites of passage' was first developed in the study of preliterate and tribal societies but has, subsequently, come to be widely used in other social contexts, including those of complex modern societies. Its popularity has occasionally led to inappropriate application which makes it all the more important to understand how the idea arose and how best to adapt and apply it in modern societies.

It was in 1908 that the Belgian anthropologist Arnold van Gennep published a study of what he called *les rites de passage*. Van Gennep belonged to a group of anthropologists including the French scholars Emile Durkheim and Marcel Mauss, whose work on ritual and beliefs was of fundamental importance for the sociology and anthropology of religion.[1] The theoretical background to his work lay in the desire to consider human action within a broad context of social life rather than as odd items of curious behaviour. He thought of anthropology as a way of interpreting apparently diverse forms of behaviour found the world over in a way that made sense of them and brought some order to what otherwise would be a confusing mass of facts. In the idea of rites of passage he believed he had discovered a key that would help unlock human behaviour, at least in the area of changing status in social life.

Van Gennep was an anthropologist who worked from the information provided by others, and he himself did not actually study peoples in other parts of the world. In *The Rites of Passage* he set himself the task of considering numerous rituals from preliterate societies in different parts of the world alongside material drawn from the sacred writings of Hindu, Jewish and Christian religions.

This was an example of the comparative method being used in anthropology as a first step to understanding human beings and their ways. The idea of 'rites of passage' is, then, a theory for interpreting changes of status in human society.

In the simplest of analogies van Gennep compared human societies with those houses that would have been so familiar to his European readers – houses possessing numerous rooms, corridors, and doors in which people live an ordinary life, moving from room to room through passages and across thresholds. By analogy, society was composed of particular social statuses with individuals passing from one status to another by passing over thresholds and moving through passages. Rites of passage were organised events in which, as it were, society took individuals by the hand and led them from one social status to another, conducting them across thresholds and holding them for a moment in a position when they were neither in one status nor another.

## The three phases of rites of passage

The overall process of movement or change in social status was seen by van Gennep as falling into three phases which mirrored the leaving of one room, then being in no room at all while in transit before finally being received into the new room. So the total ritual process was made up of three rites: the first separated people from their original status, the second involved a period apart from normal status, and the third conferred a new status upon the individual. In line with his comparison between rites of passage and movement within a house, van Gennep described these three phases of rites of passage in terms of the Latin word *limen* meaning threshold or doorstep. He spoke of the three phases as (i) pre-liminal, (ii) liminal, and (iii) post-liminal.

## Liminality

In more recent years the British anthropologist Victor Turner (1969) took up the middle phase and developed the idea of liminality by exploring the quality of relationships people have with each other during periods of change in social status. He suggested that during liminal periods individuals experience what he called a sense of *communitas*, or intense awareness of being bound together in a community of shared experience. But Turner was also very much aware that ideas applicable to those tribal and preliterate peoples traditionally studied by anthropologists are not easily transferred to modern and urban societies.

With this caution in mind, Turner (1982) still thought there were aspects of preliterate and modern life that were similar and could, with some appropriate modification, be compared. The most significant modification came when he coined the word 'liminoid' to describe periods in modern society when the ordinary system of organised activity is put aside to enable people to share in a sense of the common oneness of human existence.

## Hierarchy and *communitas*

Turner's thought works on the assumption that for much of the time societies operate a system of hierarchical and structured life where people exist with seniors above them and juniors below them and even with a degree of formal respect for their equals. But, periodically, this life of hierarchy and formal structure is interspersed with non-hierarchical and informal interaction, as though the underlying nature of being human breaks through to bring people together. He used the word *communitas* to describe the feeling which people might have while in a liminal state. Just as hierarchy divides, so *communitas* unites in many different sorts of activity. With this in mind Turner (1978) studied the place of pilgrimage, festivals, holidays and various celebrations in Christian cultures as examples of liminoid activity, as well as suggesting that monks, nuns and some others live a kind of permanently liminal life.

With the obvious exception of Islam, most of the following chapters interpret rites of passage in the narrower sense of formal change of social status from, for example, boy to man or girl to woman, from the single to the married state, from simply being married to becoming a parent, from being alive to being dead. But, in terms of Turner's theory of *liminoid* states, it would be perfectly possible to take a wider view of religions to focus on holy days and holidays, festivals and pilgrimages of many sorts.

Similarly, many examples of liminoid periods could be identified in modern societies, especially in connection with sport and entertainment. One of the most interesting and extensive liminoid moments of world history came in London in July 1985 with the Live-Aid Concert organised by the pop musician Bob Geldoff as part of an attempt to raise money and express concern for poverty-stricken areas of the world. The concert was shared by literally millions of people all over the world through the medium of satellite television. His own account of his experience at the Wembley Stadium concert on that night provides a direct description of a liminoid quality of relationships:

> Everyone came on for the finale. There was a tremendous feeling of oneness on that stage. There had been no bitching, no displays of temperament all day. Now everyone was singing. They had their arms around each other . . . everyone was crying. Not the easy tears of showbiz but genuine emotion. . . . [On the way home] . . . people walked over to the car and hugged me. Some cried, 'Oh Bob, oh Bob', not sneering, not uncontrollable, just something shared and understood. 'I know', was all I could say. I did know. I wasn't sure what had happened in England, or everywhere else, but I 'knew'. Cynicism and greed and selfishness had been eliminated for a moment. It felt good. A lot of people had rediscovered something in themselves.
>
> (Geldoff, *Is That It?*, 1986: 310)

In Turner's terms, this was a moment when the underlying humanity of many individuals was shared as distinctions of fame and celebrity faded into insignificance behind their common human nature. It was an example of that spontaneous *communitas* (described below) and shows that even when societies change and become very modern under the influence of extensive media coverage and management, the dynamics of human nature can still have a powerful effect.

## Rites and experience

Another dimension of rites of passage directly concerns the issue of personal experience or circumstances in relation to socially defined categories. Van Gennep was, for example, very clear on the fact that a gap might exist between personal circumstance and socially defined identity, as in his example that in some societies boys and girls may be deemed adult either before or after they are biologically and sexually adult. As the Christianity chapter shows, sacraments announce the status or calling of individuals while recognising that it may take some time for their self-identity and status to match each other.

## Stressing the goal

Not only did van Gennep think that rites of passage had three component rituals built into them, but he also thought that one of these three components would be emphasised depending upon the overall purpose of the ritual. So, for example, some funeral rites stress the pre-liminal aspect of separation from the land of the living, the consecration of monks or nuns might focus on a liminal existence apart from ordinary life, while marriage rites emphasise the post-liminal world of incorporation into a new family group as is very clear in the chapter on Hinduism.

Having said that, it is important to remember that rites of passage are often quite complicated and can have a variety of emphases within them. In the example of a funeral, the ritual can stress the incorporation of the deceased into the heavenly realm of the departed, while, as far as the mourners are concerned, the stress may lie on their separation from the dead.

There is another important point which emerges throughout the following chapters which, in a sense, resembles van Gennep's idea of ritual stress. It is that not all religions emphasise the same rites of passage. This is a complex issue because sometimes a particular culture utilises different religious traditions for different purposes. The chapter on Japanese religious culture makes this particularly clear in showing how people use Shinto rites in connection with birth but Buddhist rites for death. The separate chapter on Buddhism reinforces this by arguing that most life-stages are matters of secular arrangement and local custom. Death rites more directly reflect Buddhism's message of the transience of human life and the illusoriness of human identity. Christianity strongly underlines rites of incorporation into membership of the church through baptism, while Islam, for example, makes more of the place of pilgrimage as a kind of liminal separation in a mark of obedience to Allāh.

## Kinds of *communitas*

Turner identified three sorts of *communitas* which he called *spontaneous*, *ideological*, and *normative*. Spontaneous *communitas* occurs when people suddenly find themselves caught up in a shared sense of oneness. This may be because of a joy in triumph in battle, in sport, or even in a musical event like the Live-Aid Concert mentioned above. Such moments can become part of a tradition of a movement or group, so much so that it becomes an ideal. That is how Turner sees ideological *communitas*, as an ideal which reflection on past events and the wisdom of hindsight bring to a focus as a prized value. The case of the Day of Pentecost in the chapter on Christianity can be understood in this way, as an account of an experience which can come to be an ideal of Christian life which present-day congregations might seek to emulate. This is the point where ideological and normative *communitas* overlap, for normative *communitas* refers to attempts at building the ideal of spontaneity into contemporary life. Societies or groups might, for example, seek to live according to that unity of purpose outlined in a sacred text. In the Christian case, the wish to get back to the biblical form of fellowship expresses a desire for authenticity and truth which has motivated many protest movements in Christianity over the centuries. Other groups realise that history cannot be relived in this way, but might still wish to express the value of the ideal.

## Status and identity

It is important to realise that there is a distinction to be made between status and identity, a difference that van Gennep also recognised. At its simplest, status can be viewed as coming from society, as something which is accorded to an individual either because of their birth-right or else through personal achievement. Identity, by contrast, reflects the more internal process of becoming what one is supposed to be. It often takes time for the internal change to match the externally granted position.

In the western view of 'the self', a sense of identity is radically important for an individual's well-being, and forms part of what it means to be an active member of society. Identity involves our own sense of who we are in and through the various statuses we hold.

Self-identity emerges and grows as we come to grasp our various social statuses and live them out. Rites of passage often help prepare people for that sense of identity that needs to run alongside the social status accorded them. Van Gennep described how society seemed to take people by the hand, leading them from one status to another, and helping them understand themselves. The degree to which people harmonise their sense of self-identity in relation to their official social status is the degree to which they will flourish as individuals and play a creative part in the social world. Van Gennep appreciated that periods of transition between statuses was, potentially, dangerous for individuals as reflected in the caution many religions take on behalf of individuals. This is very apparent in the chapter discussing Buddhist death rites and the process of trying to assist the soul in its ongoing journey.

The importance of identity within transition rites is reflected in several chapters, on Sikhism and Judaism for example, as they discuss the new or special names given to people at times of initiation. Sometimes identity is linked to the way particular religions have their own explicit theories of life-development. This is very clearly shown in the case of Hinduism with its four stages of life.

## Reciprocity

One recurring theme of rites of passage is that of gift-giving. It is very clearly described in the following chapters for Japanese and Sikh rites but is also echoed in most of the other chapters. It is important not to ignore this rather obvious dimension of transition rituals because it helps emphasise the profoundly social nature of rites of passage.

Earlier in this introduction the names of van Gennep and Marcel Mauss were linked, as scholars committed to giving full weight to the social nature of human beings. Mauss wrote a highly influential anthropological study of gift-giving, published originally in 1925 (and translated into English in 1954). This study – *The Gift* – shows that gifts are not the free and voluntary things we often say they are; instead they are expected to be returned in some shape or form as part of ongoing networks of relationships. Reciprocal relationships of this sort are a fundamental part of life and entail mutual obligations. In rites of passage new sorts of obligations are created;

these are often marked and sustained over long periods of time through gift-giving.

## NOTES

1. Durkheim, E. (1976) *The Elementary Forms of the Religious Life* (1st edn, 1912), London, Nesbitt; Mauss, M. (1990) *The Gift* (1st edn, 1925), London, Routledge; Hubert, H. and Mauss, M. (1982) *Sacrifice: Its Nature and Function* (1st edn, 1899), Chicago, University of Chicago Press.

## FURTHER READING

Geldoff, B. (1986) *Is That It?* London, Penguin.
Gennep, A. van (1960) *The Rites of Passage* (1st edn, 1908), London, Routledge and Kegan Paul.
Golding, W. (1980) *Rites of Passage*, London, Faber.
Spencer, P. (ed.) (1990) *Anthropology and the Riddle of the Sphinx*, London, Routledge.
Turner, V. (1969) *The Ritual Process*, London, Routledge.
—— (1978) *Image and Pilgrimage in Christian Experience*, Oxford, Blackwell.
—— (1982) *From Ritual to Theatre*, New York, PAJ Publications.

# 1. Buddhism

*Christopher Lamb*

Buddhism, as a universal religion, seems remarkably deficient in rites of passage as marking in a sacred way the stages of life. There is nothing comparable with circumcision in Judaism or christening in Christianity by which a child is recognised as a member of the community, no ceremony marking the passage into adulthood, no universal ceremony of marriage. Sociologically speaking, Buddhism seems to regard marking these stages of life as a matter for secular arrangement and local custom.

Buddhism is unique among world religions in its radical denial of the existence of the self as an ontological category. Everywhere it insists on the impermanence of compounded things. Attachment to the idea of self is the primordial ignorance that holds one in bondage to *saṃsāra*, the round of rebirths. This is why Buddhist rites of passage conduct one away from the world. Victor Turner has observed this tendency in *The Ritual Process* (London, Routledge and Kegan Paul):

> Nowhere has [the] institutionalisation of liminality been more clearly marked and defined than in the monastic and mendicant states in the great world religions.
>
> (Turner 1969: 107)

## Buddhist rites and ceremonies

From the beginning Buddhism, in common with other groups of religious renouncers, did not accept the Indian *varṇāśramadharma-*

classification of the duties of life into four stages for each of the social groups. Brahminism regarded the householder-stage as an essential duty to be undertaken, but Buddhism saw this as a hindrance and treated marriage as a social contract, with no parallel to the Hindu *saṃskāra* or the Christian sacrament. Though most married Buddhists are monogamous, fraternal polyandry and even sororal polygyny have been practised in the Tibetan ethnic area. Eva Dargyay describes these in *Tibetan Village Communities* (Warminster, Aris & Phillips, 1982). Certain rituals survive from folk-religion, for example, rites of protection. Sometimes these are performed by *bhikṣus*, ordained monks, even though they have more to do with a happy continuance in the round of rebirth than liberation from it. In places, old animistic and shamanistic beliefs and practices have been adapted to the Buddhist Path to lead people's minds to faith; elsewhere, in Sri Lanka for instance, western 'values' have had their effect.

## The threefold refuge

The threefold 'going for refuge', known in Sanskrit as *Tri-śaraṇa-gamana* and in Pāli as *Ti-saraṇa-gamana*, is a ceremony used by all Buddhists, monks and laity alike, regardless of the tradition they belong to. Commonly, it is a rite of veneration of the Three Jewels, *Tri-ratna* (Pāli: *Ti-ratana*) – the Buddha, the *Dharma* and the *Saṅgha*. Also, it is the primary initiation rite by which a person enters the Middle Way and embarks on the stages of sanctification. Thereafter he or she seeks to be no longer a *pṛthagjāna* or 'common person', but to become a 'member of the family' (*gotrabhū*) of 'noble persons' (*ārya pudgalas*), eliminating all defilements on the Path to enlightenment (Akira 1990: 197–203).

The first reference to such a ceremony is ancient indeed; it occurs in the *Vinaya* (Code of Discipline) in the Pāli canon. Soon after the Buddha's enlightenment two merchants bringing rice cakes and lumps of honey approached him and then took refuge 'in the Blessed One and in the *Dhamma*'

> These were the first in the world to become lay-disciples [*upāsakas*] by the formula which contained [only] the dyad.
>
> (*Vinaya* Mv I.4.5)

As yet, the Buddha had no followers among the renouncers, so there was no *Saṅgha* or community of monks until he preached his first sermon at Sarnath. From this point the Three Jewels became the central focus of reverence in Buddhism. The first lay disciples to use the threefold formula in its present form took refuge shortly afterwards (*Vinaya* Mv I.7.10).

Nowadays laymen and women seeking to become *upāsaka*s or *upāsikā*s vow to observe Five Precepts (the first five of the ten taken by a novice monk; see p. 18) after recitation of the refuge formula. On full and new moon days they also observe Eight Precepts, taken after going for refuge. This rite is used before the *pravrajyā* (Pāli: *pabbajjā*) and *upasaṃpad* (Pāli: *upasampadā*) ceremonies of monastic ordination, and before *bodhisattva* vows are taken. In tantric ceremonies a fourth refuge in the *guru* prefaces the other three.

Van Gennep in *The Rites of Passage* (London, Routledge and Kegan Paul, 1960: 103) mentions how in Bengal an outcast becomes a Muslim to escape the hierarchy of caste. In recent times a clear example of refuge as a rite of separation is the case of the Untouchables (now called Dalits) of Pune, many thousands of whom were led by Dr Ambedkar, himself a member of the so-called Scheduled Castes, to adopt Buddhism in order to escape from low status and low self-esteem inflicted by caste Hinduism. In 1950 he headed a mass conversion of his people into Buddhism by the act of refuge.

## Meaning of the refuge ceremony

Taking refuge in the Three Jewels is what defines a Buddhist but not everyone taking it necessarily means the same thing by each of the Jewels. The Tibetan scholar Sakya Pandita in the twelfth century, differentiated between the mundane and transcendent ways of taking refuge. The mundane refuge is simply for personal advancement and welfare in present and future lives, taken by ordinary people. Whether it is taken in an inferior object, such as a god, mountain or a tree, or even in the Three Jewels, such a motivation will not bring release from *saṃsāra*. On the other hand, the transcendent way may be either common, such as the *śrāvaka*s' way, which is to attain personal liberation, or unique, such as the *bodhisattva*s' way, which is to attain the omniscience of buddhahood to help other beings. H. Saddhatissa gives a modern Theravādin interpretation in *Buddhist Ethics* (2nd edn, London, Rider, 1967).

The first Jewel is the Buddha. In the Theravāda it is emphasised that the Buddha was a man not a god. However, it would be misleading to suggest that the Buddha regarded himself as a mere man.

> Do not address, O monks, the Tathāgata [One who has gone beyond] by his name, and with the appellation 'friend'. The Tathāgata, O monks, is the holy, absolute Sambuddha [Completely awakened one].
>
> (*Vinaya* Mv I.6.12)

All schools teach that in his penultimate life a *buddha* has a divine existence as a *bodhisattva* in Tuṣita heaven. Mahayanists recognise that, along with previous earthly *buddhas*, Gautama was a manifestation of the principle of buddhahood – 'Thusness' or 'Suchness'. This idea was elaborated in the second century CE as the doctrine of the *Tri-kāya* or Three Bodies of the Buddha.

The second Jewel is the *Dharma*, which means Truth; the Truth is ultimately synonymous with the teaching of the Buddha. Teaching imparts knowledge and imposes an ethical code. Thus *Dharma* comes to mean something you can know and believe as well as something you practise; the two elements are really regarded as inseparable.

The third Jewel is the *Saṅgha*. In Theravādin countries it is usually taken in the narrow sense to indicate the monkhood in the same way that people in Britain speak of 'the Church' when they mean the clergy. In the broadest sense, however, the *Saṅgha* is the community of all who accept the teachings. Membership is formalised by taking refuge, though this is usually done before an ordained *bhikkhu* (Sanskrit: *bhikṣu*).

There is another sense in which the *Saṅgha* exists; apart from the mundane or visible community there is the *ārya-saṅgha*, the community of noble ones that cuts across the divisions of monkhood and laity. The *ārya-saṅgha* has traditionally four stages. First, there is the Stream-entrant, *śrotāpanna*, who is no longer capable of rebirth into one of the states of woe, that is as an animal, a hungry ghost or a hell-being. The next two stages refer to the prospects of rebirth, as a once-returner, *sakṛdāgāmin*, and a non-returner, *anāgāmin*. The person who achieves liberation becomes an *arhat* or *arahant*, regarded as the final stage in early Buddhism but not in the later Mahāyāna. The division between these two vehicles (*yānas*) marks an ancient argument about the altruistic interest in the salvation of others that eventually led to the rise of a new movement (Akira 1990: 256–61). The Mahāyāna's hero, the *bodhisattva-mahāsattva*, supersedes the older *arahant* and he or she settles for nothing less than liberation and buddhahood for all living things. The compassionate ideal to postpone one's own entry into *nirvāṇa*, until all others have gone before, becomes the paramount goal. In early Buddhism, where there is only one *buddha* in a world-system, the highest ideal is arahantship, never buddhahood, but in the Mahāyāna, because all things have *buddha*-nature, the difference between the teacher and the taught as an ontological category is abolished. Today the Theravāda school of Southeast Asia is the only survivor of the eighteen schools of early Buddhism.

## Method of taking refuge

The formula of refuge in Pāli is usually prefaced by a short acclamation: *namo tassa bhagavato, arahato, sammā-sambuddhassa*, 'Praise to the Blessed One, the Arahant, the Perfectly Enlightened One', repeated three times. The refuges proper then follow:

*buddhaṃ saraṇaṃ gacchāmi*
*dhammaṃ saraṇaṃ gacchāmi*
*saṅghaṃ saraṇaṃ gacchāmi*
*dutiyam pi buddhaṃ saraṇaṃ gacchāmi*
*tatiyam pi buddhaṃ saraṇaṃ gacchāmi*

I go to the Buddha for refuge
I go to the *Dharma* for refuge
I go to the *Saṅgha* for refuge
A second time I go to the Buddha for refuge, etc.
A third time I go to the Buddha for refuge, etc.

Persons taking refuge may make an offering of flowers, fruit and incense. In Thailand and other countries where they grow in abundance, it is usual to offer lotus buds. Throughout Asia the lotus, growing in muddy pools but raising its leaves and flowers above the surface of the water, symbolises the spiritual potential of humans, rooted in matter but able to transcend it. Flowers with thorns, like roses, are not considered auspicious.

Having removed their shoes, the individuals come before the *bhikkhu*, *lama* or shrine and make three obeisances or prostrations. In the Theravādin tradition they stand with their palms joined, or they kneel down and sit back on their heels. Then they raise their joined palms to their chests and bow forward to touch their foreheads on the ground. In the Tibetan tradition prostration is altogether more energetic. The joined hands are moved up from the chest to the lips, to the forehead. Prostration is done from the standing position each time and may be made in one of two ways. The first way is to raise the joined hands to the head and then fall to the knees and bow to the ground. The full prostration is performed from the standing position as before, but on sinking to the knees the whole body slides forward till it is flat on the ground. The palms are then brought together at the crown of the head and raised into the prayer position. In 1985 I myself saw dozens of people performing this devotion to the Three Jewels hundreds of times over before the main doors of the Jo-khang Temple in Lhasa. Pilgrims often measure their own length in prostrations along the route surrounding the sacred place. Atisa (1983: 24–39) gives a ritual of Sevenfold Worship of the Three Jewels.

## The fourfold refuge

Strictly speaking, the notion of the *guru* (Tibetan: *bLa-ma*), belongs to the Vajrayāna, the Diamond Vehicle, a development of the Mahāyāna, practised in Tibet and parts of China and Japan. Its religious texts are the *tantra*s (Wayman 1973); it uses *mantra*s (utterances that protect the mind), *maṇḍala*s (sacred cosmograms), ritual implements, vestments and special rituals. Teachings are given only after the disciple has received empowerment or initiation from the *guru*. The ritual complexity, richness of symbolic meaning and esoteric content make tantric initiation rites quite different from monastic ordination.

The fourfold refuge sometimes introduces purely Mahāyāna practices. The present Dalai Lama composed a *sadhana* or liturgy entitled *A Mahāyāna Method of Accomplishment: The Sadhana of the Inseparability of the Spiritual Master and Avalokiteshvara* when he was nineteen years of age. It was first printed in Tibet in 1954. Its opening lines appear also in the Tantric Ritual-Feast Offering to the Guru by the First Panchen Lama:

| | |
|---|---|
| *Namo Gurubhyaḥ* | In the Spiritual Masters I take refuge |
| *Namo Buddhāya* | In the Awakened Ones I take refuge |
| *Namo Dharmāya* | In the Truth I take refuge |
| *Namaḥ Saṅghāya* | In the Spiritual Beings I take refuge. |

There follows the refuge in the more familiar threefold form, with generating *bodhicitta*, the mind of enlightenment (Atisa: 1983: 42–63), in which the *bodhisattva* dedicates himself to working for others.

> In the Supreme Awakened One, his truth and the spiritual community
> I take refuge until becoming enlightened
> By the merit from practising giving and other perfections,
> May I accomplish Full Awakening for the benefit of all. (Three times.)

## Monastic ordination

It was not ruled out for a layperson to achieve liberation as a householder, but the early texts make it clear that once this was achieved, the new *arhat* had no alternative but to take ordination into the *Saṅgha*. Clearly, early Buddhism regarded the monastic calling as the royal road to liberation, though it needed the laity for support.

Monastic ordination is not a sacrament, but it confers a legal status which has validity in so far as it conforms with the prescriptions of the *Vinaya* and is performed by persons suitably qualified in a duly constituted quorum. In a 'central country', where there are all four classes of disciple, *bhikṣu*, *bhikṣunī*, *upāsaka*, *upāsikā*, ten monks make a quorum. For *bhikṣunī* ordinations ten nuns plus ten monks are required (except in the Mūlasarvāstivādin *Vinaya*, followed in Tibet, where ten monks and ten nuns plus one preceptress and one instructress are needed). In a 'distant country' only five of each would suffice.

The pattern of monastic ordination is more or less the same throughout Buddhism. Within the Buddha's lifetime it developed through several stages into the form we recognise today. At first the ceremony of becoming a fully ordained monk was conferred by the Buddha himself with the minimum of ceremonial. The *Vinaya* (Mv I.6.34) tells how the first five ascetics became followers after his first sermon. They requested the *pravrajyā* (Pāli: *pabbajjā*) and the *upasaṃpad* (Pāli: *upasampadā*) ordinations from the Buddha. He responded with the words:

> Come, O *bhikṣu*s, well taught is the doctrine; lead a holy life for the sake of the complete extinction of suffering.

Later he allowed monks themselves to confer ordinations:

> Let him first have his hair and beard cut off; let him put on yellow robes, adjust his upper robe so as to cover one shoulder, salute the feet of the monks with his head and sit down squatting; then let him raise his joined hands and say, 'I take my refuge in the Buddha . . . etc.'.
>
> (*Vinaya* Mv I.12.3)

Eventually the two stages of ordination were separated. A person may receive the lower ordination as a *śrāmaṇera* (Pāli: *sāmaṇera*) from eight years of age. He remains under a preceptor until the higher ordination to *bhikṣu* (Pāli: *bhikkhu*) at the age of twenty.

The Pāli rite of ordination is conducted as follows.[1]

### THE *PABBAJJĀ* (SANSKRIT: *PRAVRAJYĀ*) – LOWER ORDINATION

The candidate is presented by his preceptor, dressed as a layman but with the yellow monk's robe over his arm. After making obeisance to the assembled *bhikkhu*s he asks three times to be admitted as a *sāmaṇera* in order to destroy all sorrow, in order to attain *nibbāna*. Then he offers the robes, using the same formula. The president of the assembly takes the robes and ties the yellow band around the candidate's neck while reciting the meditation on the perishable nature of the human body. The candidate then withdraws to change into the monk's robe, meanwhile reciting a commitment to wear the robe in humility, for use and not for show. He then returns to his preceptor's side before the assembly and says:

> Grant me leave to speak. I make obeisance to my lord. Lord, forgive me all my faults. Let the merit that I have gained be shared by my lord. It is good, it is good. I share in it. Grant me leave to speak. Graciously give me, lord, the three refuges and the precepts.

He kneels and repeats the request. The preceptor leads the 'going for refuge' formula, repeated, sentence by sentence, by the candidate, and then the Ten Precepts:

> I undertake the rule of training to avoid taking life.
> I undertake the rule of training to avoid taking what is not given.
> I undertake the rule of training to avoid sexually immoral conduct.
> I undertake the rule of training to avoid false speech.
> I undertake the rule of training to avoid the use of intoxicants.
> I undertake the rule of training to avoid eating at the wrong hour.
> I undertake the rule of training to avoid dancing and worldly amusements.
> I undertake the rule of training to avoid adorning myself with garlands and scents.
> I undertake the rule of training to avoid the use of high [comfortable] beds.
> I undertake the rule of training to avoid accepting money.

The candidate then rises, makes obeisance and repeats the request that the merit should be shared by his preceptor. In return he asks to share in his preceptor's merit.

### THE *UPASAMPADĀ* (SANSKRIT: *UPASAṂPAD*) – HIGHER ORDINATION

If the candidate is to go on to be ordained a *bhikkhu* at the same ceremony the next part follows immediately. If, on the other hand, he is already a *sāmaṇera* he has to receive the *pabbajjā* ordination again before the *upasampadā* is given at the same ceremony.

Returning with his preceptor, he makes obeisance and presents an offering to the president.

> Permit me to speak. Lord, graciously grant me your sanction and support.

He kneels and requests three times more:

> Lord, be my superior.

The president says:

> It is well,

and the candidate responds:

> I am content. From this day forth my lord is my charge. I am charge to my lord. (Repeated three times.)

The candidate rises and, after making obeisance, returns alone to the foot of the assembly where the alms bowl is strapped to his back. His preceptor then goes down to him and leads him back by the hand. A monk from the assembly stands and places himself beside the candidate on the other side from the preceptor. The two then with the permission of the assembly question the candidate as to his fitness:

> Your name is N——?
> It is so, my lord.
> Your preceptor is the venerable N——?
> It is so, my lord.
> Praise be to the Blessed One, the Arahant, the supremely enlightened Buddha.

They then enquire whether the candidate has an alms bowl and robes. He then retires backwards to the foot of the assembly where he is examined concerning his fitness (i.e., freedom from certain impediments such as diseases, that he is a human male, not required for military service, not a debtor, has parental permission, is of the full age of twenty years, and so on). When satisfactory answers have been given the preceptors request the president for permission to tell the candidate to approach. He comes forward to stand between the preceptors, makes obeisance and kneels, to say:

> Monks, I ask the assembly for ordination; Monks, have compassion on me and raise me up. (Repeated three times)

The preceptors examine the candidate again concerning his freedom from impediments. This is the examination in the midst of the assembly. One of the preceptors reports that the candidate desires ordination under the venerable N——, is free from impediments, has alms bowl and robe intact. He then says:

> The candidate asks the assembly for ordination under his preceptor the venerable N——. The assembly gives ordination under his preceptor the venerable N——. If anyone approves the ordination of the candidate under the venerable N——, let him remain silent; if any objects, let him speak. (Repeated three times).

The preceptors make obeisance and say:

> The candidate has received ordination as a *bhikkhu* under his preceptor the venerable N——. The assembly approves the resolution: therefore it keeps silence. So I understand your wish.

After each candidate has been ordained in turn, the group of newly ordained *bhikkhu*s is instructed in keeping the full 227 rules of the *Vinaya*.

The training of a Zen Buddhist monk (Suzuki 1934: 3–13) opens with a period of harsh austerity spent on the threshold of the community (the liminal stage) that tests his will to persevere to the utmost before he is given admittance. The aspirant must present himself at the door with a certificate saying he is a regularly ordained disciple (the preliminal stage) of a Zen priest, who will have tonsured him and provided his *kesa* and *koromo* (priestly robes), a razor, a set of bowls, some money for his burial in case of unexpected death; all these objects are carried in a papier-mâché box suspended from his neck by a sash.

Dressed in cotton leggings and wearing a broad bamboo hat and straw sandals, the novice presents himself at the porch of the monastery. He is firmly refused entry on some pretext such as that the *zendo* is full. He meets further refusal and is left alone. He must persevere by remaining crouched over his baggage. Sometimes he is physically ejected beyond the gate. There he sits in meditation until nightfall. He may be invited inside, but not to sleep. Instead, he is shown into a room where he must sit facing the wall in meditation. When morning comes he must gather his bags and return to the porch to crouch over them. This period of *niwa-dzume* (occupying the entrance court) might last three days. After this he is allowed to come inside and pass another three days isolated in a room, spending all day in meditation. Finally, he is advised that he is to be admitted into the *zendo*. He puts on his *kesa* (robe) and is ushered in by a monk to pay homage to the image of Mañjuśrī. He spreads his *zagu* (meditation cloth) and prostrates three times. His admission is announced and a tea ceremony follows. A few days later he is introduced to the master. At the threshold he spreads his *zagu* on it, makes three bows and offers incense. A tea ceremony follows. At the evening *sanzen* he will gather with the other monks before the master in the Rinzai sect of Zen, and receive his *koan*. Thus his life as a monk begins (incorporation stage).

## The establishment of the order of nuns

Mahaprajapati, the Buddha's aunt and step-mother, succeeded after much perseverance to get herself and her companions ordained as nuns (*bhikṣunīs*). However, they were required to keep the Eight Strict Rules (*garudhammā*) in addition to all the other precepts kept by fully ordained monks. These are as follows:

1. A nun even of 100 years' standing shall salute a monk and rise up even if he is only newly ordained.
2. A nun shall not spend retreat in a place where there is no monk.
3. Twice monthly the nuns shall ask for the time of the *Uposatha* ceremonies (when the disciplinary code is recited and fully ordained members undertake thorough self-examination) from the monks and the time when a monk will come to preach.

4. The final Retreat ceremony is to be held by the nuns in both the monks' and the nuns' *saṅgha*s.
5. Certain offences are to be declared before both *saṅgha*s.
6. A novice after training in the six rules for two years shall ask for ordination from both *saṅgha*s.
7. A nun is forbidden to rebuke or abuse a monk on any pretext.
8. Nuns are forbidden to address monks but it is not forbidden for monks to address nuns.

(*Vinaya* Cu.X)

Apart from the eight extra *prātimokṣa* rules, the *Vinaya* prescribes an additional two-year period which nuns must serve as a *śikṣamāṇā* (probationer) after the *śrāmaṇerikā* stage, before receiving the higher ordination to *bhikṣunī*. The *śikṣamāṇā* receives six precepts additional to the ten precepts of the novice.

The *bhikṣunī* lineage was transmitted from India to Sri Lanka by Sanghamitta, the daughter of the Emperor Asoka who lived about 272–236 BCE. In 429 CE and 433 CE two groups of Sri Lankan *bhikṣunī*s went to China. The *bhikṣunī* lineage died out in Sri Lanka probably in the late tenth century (Gombrich and Obeyesekere 1988: 274). Apart from any natural difficulties for women leading the homeless life, what other factors may have caused it to die out? The ordination of a nun required a double ceremony; first she was to be ordained by the *bhikṣunī-saṅgha* and then by the *bhikṣu-saṅgha*. There were some countries in the Buddhist world where the full ordination of nuns was never introduced. In Tibet women were ordained as *śrāmaṇerika*s (novices) but the order of *bhikṣunī*s was never introduced. It is more surprising that *bhikṣunī*s were never introduced into Thailand, though the lineage existed in Burma (Myanmar) during the Pagan period from the eleventh century until the Mongol invasions in the thirteenth.

In modern times there have been moves, largely led by Westerners, to reintroduce the order into the Theravāda and to introduce it for the first time into the Tibetan tradition from the Chinese *bhikṣunī* order that follows the Dharmaguptaka *Vinaya* to this day. Since the Chinese nuns got their lineage from Sri Lanka originally, there is a strong argument for reintroduction, even though the modern Chinese nuns are Mahāyānists. What matters is that the *prātimokṣa* (Pāli: *pātimokkha*) rules of *Vinaya* should have been correctly kept and transmitted according to the tradition laid down in the *Vinaya sūtras*. In Tibet, *śrāmaṇas* and *śrāmaṇerakis* wear the same robes as *bhikṣus*, that is maroon with a yellow ceremonial outer robe, but in Southeast Asia women are not commonly seen in the yellow robe. There they more usually wear white or brown. They are regarded as lay by the Thai state.

## Tantric initiation or empowerment – *abhiṣeka*

Before practising on the third vehicle, the Vajrayāna, it is necessary to receive a permission or empowerment (*abhiṣeka*, Tibetan: *dbang-bksur*) from a master who has received his own empowerment in a direct line back to the Buddha himself. Initiates in all classes of tantra become *bodhisattvas*, if they are not already so, by taking the *bodhisattva* vows (Atisa 1983: 88–109). In the Yoga and the Highest Yoga classes, extra tantric vows are taken besides vows specific to one of the five *buddha*-families that the initiate is to join when he or she enters the *maṇḍala*.

The stages preliminary to initiation include the request of the disciples to the *guru*, the rituals for preparing the site of the ceremony, preparations for the construction of the *maṇḍala*, analysis of the *guru*'s dreams to ensure that the conditions are propitious, actual construction of the *maṇḍala*, and veiling the *maṇḍala*. At this point a tantric dance may be performed. At the next stage the initiates request initiation, take the *bodhisattva* and tantric vows and receive a blessing of their body, speech and mind with consecrated water. Each receives from the *guru* two sheaves of kusha grass and a red protection string with instruction to sleep in the same posture as the Buddha at death (i.e., on the right side). Dreams reported to the *guru* next day are analysed and the *guru* stands to make a prophecy as a *buddha*, that the initiates will one day achieve enlightenment. It is a prophecy from which no one can be excluded, because every *bodhisattva* vows not to enter *nirvāṇa* till every sentient being has gone before, so, in that sense, no one is liberated until everyone is liberated.

The initiates wear blindfolds of red cloth. They cast a flower into the *maṇḍala*; the place where it falls establishes the *buddha*-family to which they belong. They receive a tantric name and then remove the blindfold to view the *maṇḍala*. Alex Wayman (1973: 62) explains that the actual procedures are often different from what is read about them. For example, the blindfold is not worn over the eyes but around the forehead. The petal of the *champa* flower (which had earlier been thrown into the *maṇḍala*) is not worn 'as a garland' but pasted in the middle of the forehead after the 'blindfold' has been removed. The blindfold is not so much to conceal the *maṇḍala* from the uninitiated as to symbolise the former blindness of primordial ignorance and the opening of the third wisdom-eye.

The Highest Yoga *tantra*s generally have four initiations or consecrations: the Vase or Jar, the Secret, the Wisdom-gnosis and the Word or 'Fourth'. The Vase consecration gives permission to practise the Generation stage and the three later consecrations apply to the Completion stage.[2] Only a brief outline of Generation stage consecrations can be attempted here. For a close account of these see Tenzin Gyatso, the Dalai Lama and Jeffrey Hopkins in *The Kālachakra Tantra: Rite of Initiation for the Generation Stage* (London, Wisdom Publications, 1985: 257–353).

## The Jar consecration

This consecration is normally sub-divided into water, crown, *vajra* (sceptre), bell and name initiations for the Yoga and Highest Yoga *tantra*s. Each of the consecrations corresponds to one of the five Wisdoms; e.g., water to the Mirror-like Wisdom of Akṣobhya, crown to the Wisdom of Sameness of Ratnasambhava, *vajra* to the Discriminating Wisdom of Amitābha, bell to the All-accomplishing Wisdom of Amoghasiddhi, name to the Wisdom of the pure Absolute of Vairocana.

The royal associations of these consecrations cannot be missed; water brought from all the sacred rivers of India was used for royal anointings in ancient times. The crown refers not only to a royal diadem but to the *uṣṇīṣa*, the bump on the head of a *buddha*. This betokens wisdom and is one of the thirty-two marks of a *mahā-puruṣa*, a person destined to be either a fully enlightened *buddha* (*saṃyaksambuddha*) or a universal monarch (*cakravartin*). The *vajra* is the diamond-hard indestructible truth; it is also the thunderbolt of Indra, a royal sceptre. The bell initiation is additionally known as the Sovereign or the Royal consecration.

## Folk Buddhism – accommodations for the 'stages of life'

As a result of its refusal to concern itself directly with the stages of worldly life, Buddhism has left the lay Buddhist somewhat unprovided for. However, Buddhism has usually been tolerant towards pre-Buddhist indigenous religions. They have sometimes been left to provide those rites that Buddhism does not provide, as, for example, in Japan, where people generally marry by Shinto rites but have a Buddhist funeral. One of the clearest examples of Buddhism adapting its own institutions to meet a gap in the provision of rites of passage may be seen in countries of Southeast Asia, such as Thailand, Myanmar (Burma), Laos and Cambodia. Here laymen often spend brief periods of their lives observing the Ten Precepts as novice monks. The first time a boy takes the robe the ceremony is performed with great splendour. His family dresses him in royal robes and a golden crown. As Śākyamuni Buddha himself gave up rank and possessions to take up the homeless life, so the boy puts off his finery, has his head shaved and is dressed in the yellow robe. He receives the lower ordination and must keep the Ten Precepts for a week or two. The ceremony marks a stage in the child's development when be becomes capable of spiritual and moral discernment. From another point of view the ordination shows that, however tender in years or however old the candidate is, the spiritual ideal is the same for all, with no special duties for each stage of life. From the outset Buddhism formally did away with caste, hence every Buddhist child may wear royal robes, in order to discard them for the yellow robe, which itself bestows a status higher than royalty.

Mary Shepherd Slusser, in her cultural study of the Kathmandu Valley, *Nepal Mandala* (2 vols), Princeton, Princeton University Press, 1982: 294–8), has observed a form of Vajrayāna Buddhism that is practised alongside Hinduism. For historical and social reasons the celibate monkhood died out but it was never entirely forgotten. It has given rise to a strange phenomenon in the Newar community – two dynasties of married 'monks'. Children of the Buddhist priestly Vajrācārya caste, whose ancestors were probably tantric *yogins*, possibly with brahman connections, and the Śākyabhikṣus, who belong to the same clan as Śākyamuni Buddha himself, and whose ancestors were once monks, receive the rite of tonsure. This rite has become a kind of *saṃskāra* by which they become ‘monks’; in the case of the Vajrācāryas, priests also. The ceremony must be performed in the same *vihāra* in which it was done for the boy’s ancestors. Nowadays the rites are performed on groups of candidates, who might be mere babes in arms, boys or youths. They present themselves, fasting, for a ritual bath and head shaving. Then they are given the yellow robe, staff and begging bowl. They remain as monks for four days and then return to the *vihāra* to renounce the robe formally.

A Vajrācārya boy receives further investitures of the *yogin*’s *vajra* and bell. If he does not complete this rite he forfeits his status as a priest not only for himself but for his descendants as well. Thereafter they would have only *bhikṣu* status.

Other variations and adaptations of ordinations occur. In parts of China the practice of moxibustion (lighting of cones of herbs on the skin for curative purposes) was combined with the ordination rites of monks. In such a case, five cones were placed on the head of the ordinand, perhaps for their therapeutic value but also as a metaphor of the curative nature of the Noble Truths as diagnosis, aetiology, prognosis and medicament. Extreme asceticism in another form is practised by the monks of Mount Hiei in Japan who undertake to complete certain marathon pilgrimages up the holy mountain. If they succeed they are revered as living *buddha*s, but if they fail they must commit ritual suicide. Generally suicide is disapproved of in Buddhism, though in the *Jātaka* Tales, stories of the former lives of the Buddha, there are several accounts of the *bodhisattva* laying down his life out of compassion for other beings. Ritual self-immolation, as practised by monks during the Vietnamese war, will be discussed below (p. 36)

## Buddhist marriage

Usually Buddhism has not regarded the institution of marriage as sacred in any way. However, in Sri Lanka the influence of colonial and missionary activities brought about a change in the traditional practice of Buddhist marriage as part of a larger reaction that Gombrich and Obeyesekere (1988: 255–73) have called Protestant Buddhism. Up to this period both polygyny and polyandry were practised in Sinhala villages, and divorce was easy to obtain. In a typical marriage that took place at the beginning of the nineteenth century, the bridegroom came with his relations to the bride's parents' house. A white cloth was spread out over a plank and fresh rice was scattered on it. The bride's maternal uncle then placed the bride and groom on the plank. The bridegroom gave the bride gifts of a gold chain, a cloth and a jacket, followed by an exchange of rings. To the bride's mother he gave a white cloth. Then the uncle tied the couple's thumbs together. A plate was held under their joined thumbs and some milk poured over the knot. Sometimes the couple's little fingers were joined instead of their thumbs, and in some places the groom put the chain around the bride's neck. There was no religious officiant, nor were religious texts recited. In fact, the presence of a monk, who was dedicated to celibacy and so seen as asexual, would have been inauspicious for the fertility of the union. The giving of gifts and the wedding banquet were to mark the bringing together of two kin-groups. Only one element in the marriage ritual seems to have been common; the giving of the white cloth by the groom to his new mother-in-law. A white cloth is also given by the relatives of the deceased to the monks who officiate at a funeral. In both cases the cloth symbolically absorbs pollution. The white cloth is worn by the bride on her wedding night and this cloth absorbs the pollution of sexual intercourse.

The ceremony of the plank (*pōruva*) has now become universal in the marriage ceremony. The *pōruva* is a flat board used in preparing the seed-bed of paddy fields; sprinkling it with rice grains in the context of the marriage ceremonial symbolises the fertility of the union. Nowadays it is decorated to resemble a throne, certainly in urban upper-class weddings, and though the term *pōruva* is still used, its fertility associations seem to have been forgotten. The royal associations are reinforced by the sumptuous wedding clothes of the bride and groom.

White is a colour used to absorb impurity; it is both the colour of mourning and the colour of chastity, worn by those who have taken Eight or Ten precepts and so is associated with sterility. It seems odd, therefore, that Buddhist brides should have increasingly taken to wearing white, but in order to sacramentalise marriage within the context of Buddhism, certain features of the Christian rite have provided the model. Little girls dressed as bridesmaids chant a medieval Pāli text, the *Jayamangala Gāthā*, following the *pōruva* ceremony. The text has nineteen four-line stanzas, each one celebrating a victory of the Buddha. The irony of this is probably missed by the wedding guests who would only recognise the words *jaya* (victory) and *mangala* (auspiciousness). Gombrich and Obeyesekere relish the irony that the theme of the text is the triumph of ascetic renunciation over sex and procreation, sung by pre-pubescent girls dressed in sterile white!

By the mid-1970s, not only had monks made occasional appearances at weddings, but some had even solemnised them in temples. After the *pōruva* ceremony the monks chant *pirit*. The Sinhala word *pirit* (Pāli: *paritta*), originally meaning 'amulet', denotes a group of texts which are recited in a ritual to avert misfortune. A thread is held by the monks reciting *pirit* and passed around to contain all the people present, any of whom may also hold the thread. A bottle of water is placed under the table holding the texts during the recitation. Everyone is sprinkled with the water after the end of the recitation. Gombrich (1971: 201–9), in addition to describing it fully, considers some of the doctrinal anomalies in the practice.

The most recent development is the introduction of a special wedding celebrant who operates rather like a brahman priest. In one such case Gombrich and Obeyesekere (1988: 269) observed 'the Buddhicization of the previously secular ceremony'; a brief outline of their complete description is all that can be given here. The celebrant opens with a formal request of permission to perform the marriage from the Buddha, *Dhamma* and *Saṅgha*, and also from the gods, parents and congregation. Prior to the *pōruva* ceremony, the celebrant utters an exposition of the 'original' Buddhist marriage between the then Prince Siddhartha (the future Buddha) and Yasodhara, in the presence of all the great gods. The god Īśvara provided a *pirit* thread and tied the fingers of the couple. The god Brahmā poured water over their hands and by this they were brought to liberation. The celebrant then sings the last stanzas of the *pirit*. The *pōruva* ceremony now follows. The groom, after asking permission from the authorities listed before, places a ring on the bride's fourth finger of her left hand. The other ceremonies of the necklace and the white cloth follow. It is the father of the bride (not her maternal uncle, as used to be done in the villages) who ties the couple's fingers while the celebrant gives a blessing:

> By the influence of all the glorious Buddhas, Pacceka [solitary] Buddhas, and Arhats I secure your protection in every way.

The father pours *pirit* water over their hands and the bridesmaids sing the *Jayamangala Gāthā*. The couple give food to each other and give a betel leaf to relations and guests. When the couple descend from the *pōruva*, a coconut is smashed before them to banish the evil eye, mouth and thoughts, and to obtain the blessing of Gaṇeśa and the Earth Goddess. They light a lamp for the Buddha and go to sign the marriage register.

In the Himalayan regions, among the ethnic Tibetans, marriages are sometimes played out as a kind of symbolic 'kidnapping'. The poorer party is kidnapped by the richer. This usually means the man's family does the kidnapping, but not invariably. The one who is abducted, woman (or man), sobs while she (or he) is being led to the groom's (or bride's) house. In former times marriages were arranged by the parents within classes, but since the invasion of Tibet social stratification has become less rigid. At various stages of arrangement and engagement white silk scarves are presented by the man's family to the woman's. She is also presented with a striped apron which forms part of a married woman's dress, and a marriage contract is drawn up in duplicate.

On the wedding morning the groom sends a representative on horseback with a retinue, carrying the headgear, coloured arrows decorated with mirrors, and jade ornaments, to the bride for her wedding attire. Before they arrive she makes a grain offering and drinks *chang* (barley beer). The groom's representative enters her house, fixes the arrows to her back to show that she has now changed over to the groom's family and places the jade ornament on her head to indicate that she has charge of the groom's spirit. If one is available, the bride rides back on a mare in foal. As she leaves, one of her family on the roof of the house, holding an arrow and a leg of mutton, repeatedly cries out after them: 'Do not take away our family's good fortune'. The bridal party is met by members of her new family offering refreshments at three points on the route.

At the bridegroom's house the bride dismounts on to a mat made of bags of barley and wheat covered in brocaded silk. A swastika is formed out of sprinkled barley grains on top of the mat. As the bride crosses into her husband's household an auspicious omen might be read and blessings given. Tadeusz Skorupski has translated such a rite, an example of the accommodation of Buddhist ceremony mixed with animistic ritual to the secular rite of marriage, in 'A Tibetan

Marriage Ritual' (*The Journal of Asian and African Studies*, No. 31, 1986: 76–95). In outline there are eight parts to the ritual:

1. The elimination of evil *'dre* who precede the bride: this is effected by the powers of the Buddhist religion:

   > By the truth of the noble lamas of Buddhist religion,
   > The truth of the Buddha, his Doctrine and Community [i.e., the Three Jewels]
   > The truth of the secret *mantra*s, *vidhyā*s, *dharaṇī*s and *mudrā*s,
   > The truth of the Absolute Sphere, pure and free of cause and effect,
   > In particular by the truth of the Peaceful and Wrathful Deities
   > Who have assumed manifestations as Mañjuśrī,
   > The truth of the noble and holy Religion-Protectors,
   > Those of the highest and worldly ranks.
   > And by the blessing of the Great Truth.

2. The purification of the bride: because the household deities are liable to be polluted by the new bride, she must be purified by pouring water in front of a mirror in which an image of a deity is reflected on to the bride. Her purity will now be the same as that of the deity.
3. The spreading of the carpet: the preface to the spreading of the carpet which promotes the bride's life-force, power and good luck refers to the legend by which the two Buddhist wives, one Chinese and one Nepali, of the king Srong-btsan sgam-po landed in Central Tibet on a magic carpet.
4. The presentation of the three white things: milk, curds and butter to give long life.
5. The bestowal of the new name.
6. The presentation to the house deities: holding a garlanded arrow which has a complex symbolism, the officiant presents the bride to the house deities and asks that 'the body, speech and mind of this noble maiden be protected, defended and blessed' by many deities of all kinds, including the four *tantra*s and the benign host of peaceful and wrathful deities, for example, Vajravārāhī, the white Tārā, five classes of *ḍākinī*s, and more.
7. The rite of summoning good fortune.
8. The final prayer invokes on the bride the blessing of 'victorious lamas and their spiritual sons', 'hermits who follow the truth',

and the Three Jewels. It asks that the 'celestial constellations . . . be auspicious', 'the Buddhas display . . . miraculous powers' and 'the Arhats annihilate misery'.

## The ceremonies of death

In an early account in the Pāli canon the *Mahāparinibbāna sutta* tells that just before his death the Buddha gave instructions to the monk Ananda on how his funeral rites were to be conducted according to elaborate rites for the cremation of a universal monarch (*cakravartin*). A *stūpa* was to be raised over the relics at a crossroads. However, the monks were to hand over the funeral arrangements to the laity.

> Do not worry yourselves about the funeral arrangements, Ānanda. You should strive for the highest goal, devote yourselves to the highest goal, and dwell with your minds tirelessly, zealously devoted to the highest goal. There are wise Khattiyas, Brahmans and householders who are devoted to the Tathāgata: they will take care of the funeral.
>
> (*Dīgha nikāya* 16.5.10)

Though we do not know how soon after the Buddha's own funeral monks began the custom, in modern Sri Lanka Theravādin monks take part in funerals. The presence of monks at funerals technically would not be to do anything for the dead person – certainly not to pray for him or her. A funeral is a reminder of mortality and impermanence and it is quite appropriate that monks should take the opportunity to preach *buddhadharma* out of compassion for the bereaved. Monks are formally given food a week after the death, three months later and then on the anniversary at a commemorative ceremony. One of the chief ways by which the laity gain merit (for an auspicious rebirth, ideally, from which to reach *nirvāṇa*) is by offering food to monks, either at the daily almsround or by inviting monks for meals. In the case of the dead, the merit gained by the relatives is thought to be transferable to the dead person (Gombrich 1971: 232–40).

At the funeral itself a white cloth is laid on the coffin. A monk leads the taking of refuge in the Three Jewels and the Five Precepts. Then he says three times, repeated by all present:

I give this corpse-clothing to the *Saṅgha* of monks.

The monks spread the cloth over the coffin and chant a stanza spoken first at the death of the Buddha:

Impermanent indeed are compounded things, prone to rise and fall,
Having risen, they're destroyed, their passing truest bliss.

(*Dīgha nikāya* 16.6.10).

The monks pick up the white cloth which has symbolically absorbed the pollution of the corpse; they are immune from it. It also symbolises, quite separately, an optional ascetic practice whereby monks could make their robes from cloths discarded on dust-heaps or in cremation grounds. The outer robe of a monk today is still made up of pieces of cloth stitched together, even if they have been cut from the same bolt of new cloth. Though this is supposed to destroy the 'value' of the cloth and any ensuing hubris a monk might have in wearing it, the patchwork finish is also a reminder of the way the earliest renouncers came by their robes.

Following removal of the cloth, water is poured from a jug into a bowl until it overflows (or a coconut is split to spill its milk) while the monks chant the following verses:

As the full water-bearing [rivers] fill the ocean,
so indeed does what is given here benefit the dead (*preta*).

As water rained on a height reaches the low land,
so indeed does what is given here benefit the dead (*preta*).

A sermon is preached and the monks usually depart, leaving the relatives to conclude the actual burial or cremation, possibly to conform with the precedents of the Buddha's funeral.

Normally the feast (*dānē*) for the dead person is rigorously observed on the seventh day after death. The one three months later, and the anniversary, while not being obligatory, are commonly observed. Sometimes monks give *dānē* for their parents or predecessors. The donor gives food to the monk, who recites a Pāli verse and dedicates the merit.

The invitation to the *dānē* for the seventh day is given to the *saṅgha* rather than to an individual monk. Usually a minimum of five is expected, though poor people may invite fewer and rich people more. A sermon is preached on the evening before and the monks are invited to eat in the donor's home. On this occasion only the relatives and closest friends attend. The three-month *dānē* is a semi-public affair to which all who knew the deceased are invited. It usually starts with *pirit*. The food is offered with the Pāli formula, repeated three times:

> I give this alms-food to the community of monks.

A little food is put outside for the *preta*s (hungry ghosts – along with animals and hell-beings – making up the three woeful destinies one can be reborn to). This tradition of feeding the *preta*s is found throughout Buddhism; food is put out for *preta*s during the tantric liturgical feast-offering to the *Guru* (*bLa-ma chos-pa*).

After food the monks may be offered small gifts; then a bowl and a jug of water are set before them. The donor pours water into the dish until it overflows, as was done at the funeral. When the chant and water-pouring are over the people say '*Sā*' (Pāli: *sādhu*, 'it is good'). A short sermon on impermanence is given and then the donor transfers the merit of the actions to the dead by means of a formula recited in Pāli that means:

> May this be for my relatives. May my relatives be happy.

The canonical precedent for these ceremonies is found in *Anguttara nikāya* (V. 269–73).

In Tibet funeral rites are unusually varied; corpses may be disposed of by 'sky' burial, water burial, earth burial, cremation or by being placed in a *stūpa*, according to the status of the dead person. Prior to the burial, whatever form it is to take, a period of preparation must be undertaken to help the dead person come to terms with his or her new state. The body, covered by a white cloth, is laid out and the ceremony of reading the *Bar-do Thos-grol* into the ear of the dead person for a period of three to five days is undertaken by monks. This text guides the newly departed through the celebrated *bar-do* state, made famous by Evans-Wentz's publication of a translation of the *Tibetan Book of the Dead* (3rd edn, repr. Oxford University Press, 1985). In the Tibetan and some Far Eastern traditions, but not in the Theravāda – though Ven.

Rahula connects the seventh day *dānē* with it (Gombrich 1971: 232) – there is a belief in an intermediate state between death and rebirth lasting between seven and forty-nine days. The ceremony of reading may be begun before death if the person is mortally ill. Relatives and friends come to pay their respects and bring gifts for the grieving family and a ceremonial white silk scarf for the deceased. All ornaments of the house are put away, the family do not wash their faces or comb their hair during the period of mourning. No person touches the corpse, in order to allow the *bar-do* body to separate itself from the material body. This might be helped by a *'pho-bo*, an officiant who attempts to extract the consciousness principle. He commands the consciousness to give up its attachment to its now-defunct body, its living relatives and goods. He draws out a few hairs above the 'Aperture of Brahmā' at the line of the sagittal suture on the top of the skull to aid the departure of consciousness.

Next the body is stripped, the knees are drawn up to the chest and bound in the embryonic posture. Then the body is wrapped in a woollen blanket. Disposal of the body takes place when it is certain that separation of body and consciousness have taken place. Until that time the mourners are fed and a portion of food and drink is offered to the deceased spirit. After the funeral proper has been carried out an effigy of the dead person is placed in the room and offered food for the full forty-nine days of the *bar-do*; the number of days is said to correspond to the period of the Buddha's awakening.

During the funeral rites and reading of the *Bar-do Thos grol*, other monks in relays chant a text to help the deceased reach the Western Paradise of Amitābha (Sukhāvatī). The corpse is carried to the door of the house and placed on the back of the undertaker to be taken to the place of burial. The procession is led by a lama who holds one end of the white scarf which has been tied to the body.

The commonest form of funeral for ordinary folk, sky burial, may have been influenced by the Iranian practice of exposing the dead in Towers of Silence. The body is taken up to a high outcrop of rock and a fire of cypress wood lit. *Tsam-pa* (roasted barley flour) is sprinkled on and the smoke signals to the sacred vultures to assemble. The flesh is cut from the corpse in pieces and heaped on one side; then the bones are crushed and mixed with *tsam-pa*. This is fed to the vultures before the flesh so that every part of the body is consumed. It is regarded as a very bad omen if the vultures do not complete their task or are scared off. The Chinese authorities have now stopped tourists in Lhasa disturbing the sacred birds from their meal with flashlight photography.

Water burial is used for beggars, destitutes and the widowed; earth burial is for robbers, murderers and those who die of leprosy and smallpox; cremation is for the nobility and higher-ranking monks. Possibly the first time cremation in the Tibetan manner was done in the West was for Lama Yeshe, a Geshe in exile who inaugurated the Foundation for the Preservation of the Mahāyāna Tradition (FPMT). The ceremony was conducted in 1984 near Boulder Creek in California, using the Yamāntaka fire *pūjā*. The body was placed in the *stūpa* with the knees drawn up and tied with white scarves. The arms were crossed and a *vajra* and bell were placed in the hands. Upon the head was placed a black *bodhisattva*'s hat adorned with a crystal rosary. A red cloth was placed over the face. The *stūpa*, made of bricks covered in mud and whitewash, was built up round the body. Wood was stacked around and oil poured over it. There were four holes around the base and two more for receiving offerings on the upper part. The fire had to be kindled by someone who had not received the Lama's teachings.

The highest kind of burial, inurnment in a *stūpa*, is reserved for the highest lamas, such as the Dalai and Tashi Lamas. The corpse is mummified with salt and spices, covered in a cement-like substance, covered in gold and the face-part painted. There are funeral halls holding the mummies of former Dalai and Tashi Lamas in the Po-tala palace, Lhasa, and in the Tashilhunpo monastery at Shigatse.

Mummification may seem an incongruous practice in face of the Buddhist insistence on the transience of the person. Corpses in cremation grounds may be used for meditation on impermanence, but they are unstable and have to be disposed of quite quickly; indeed, the fact that they do decompose is the very point of the contemplation. Skeletons and even stillborn babies in formalin may occasionally be seen in wats in Thailand, but their purpose is undoubtedly different from the veneration of mummies that seems to have emerged as such an important feature of Ch'an/Zen. (*Chan* is the Chinese pronunciation of Sanskrit *dhyāna* (meditation); *zen* is the Japanese pronunciation of *chan*. These Far Eastern developments of Buddhism emphasised 'sudden' enlightenment, in contrast to the 'gradual' enlightenment of the Indian schools.) Here the point of this contemplation is the body of a *buddha*. In his critique of the ritualisation of death in Chan/Zen, Bernard Faure (1991: 134) argues that the production of *śarīra* (crystalline fragments left from cremation) and 'flesh-body' (mummy) can both be classified as 'secondary burial', the goal of which was to obtain an incorruptible body. As in the West, relics, though they could be handled, 'belonged not to the transitory world but to eternity'. 'Self-mummification' is a very slow fast to death, bringing about a virtual dessication; this and self-immolation probably attempt the same goal through different funerary practices.

## Ritual suicide

The *Lotus Sūtra*, written in India in the first century CE, may have inspired the practice of ritual self-immolation, though only in the Far East. Walpola Rahula says:

> The monk who prepared himself for self-cremation gradually reduced his intake of cereals and partook of incense, perfume and oil. After a period he became emaciated and his body was, therefore, more combustible. It was then both a lamp-offering and an incense-offering.
>
> . . . A niche large enough for a person to sit cross-legged was prepared in the middle of the pyre. The hero-monk entered the niche, sat cross-legged, set fire to the pyre himself, and with palms folded in salutation to the Buddha recited a sacred text (such as the *Amitābha-sūtra*) calmly and serenely until he died.
>
> (*Zen & the Taming of the Bull*, London, Gordon Fraser, 1978: 113)

The first recorded case of self-mummification was a monk of Dunhuang who died in 385 CE after a seven-year fast (Faure 1991: 158). At first these 'relics' were abandoned in mountain caves but at the beginning of the T'ang period, when Zhiyi the founder of the T'ian-t'ai school died, his mummy was enshrined in a memorial hall. Incorruptibility came to be seen as the result of impregnation by morality, concentration and wisdom, tokens that the hero would be reborn in Amitābha Buddha's Pure Land.

## Funerary rituals in Chan/Zen

The shift in Ch'an/Zen from being a 'self-power' philosophy of life to funerary ritualism, reliant on 'other power' of Amitābhism, seems to have dated from the fourteenth century. Faure says of the early Ch'an ideology of death:

> Reinforcing the no-self theory of early Buddhism, the Mahāyāna doctrine, as exemplified by the *Heart Sūtra*, further blunted the scandal of death by denying its ontological reality; in emptiness (*śūnyatā*) there is neither birth nor death, neither coming nor going. Accordingly temporality and finitude were ultimately negated as karmic delusions.
>
> (Faure, 1991: 180)

The first effect of this was to lead to the theoretical rejection of funeral rites; one patriarch, Fachi (637–702) of the Niutou school, ordered his corpse to be left to wild animals so that they would absorb his virtue and produce the thought of enlightenment (*bodhicitta*). But eventually, as a 'skilful means' (*upāya*), or a synthesis with the old ancestor worship, funerary rituals became firmly rooted.

The ritual preliminaries of the death of a Chan master from early times began with the prediction of the precise time of death, closely modelled on the Buddha's own *parinirvāṇa* (Faure 1991: 184). On New Year's Eve one covers the ears with both hands and knocks the skull for the number of months and days in the coming year. When the point is reached where there is no sound, that is the day of one's death.

The Chan master's next task was to compose his 'death verse' (*gāthā*). Very rarely he refused to comply; or he expressed reservations:

> Life's as we
> Find it – death too.
> A parting poem?
> Why insist?
>
> Daie-Soko (1089–1163)

The death of a master became a public event and so it was necessary that he should meet his end reclining on his right side like the Buddha or seated in the lotus posture of *samādhi*.

Funerals of monks who had reached enlightenment were different from those of ordinary monks. These last eventually became the model for laypeople in Japan. A master's funeral had nine rites: placing the body in a coffin; transferring the coffin to the lecture hall; closing the coffin; placing a portrait of the master on the shrine; the wake; removal to the cremation ground; offering a tea libation; offering a hot water libation; lighting the pyre. The rites at all stages were accompanied by tea offerings, chanting of *dhāraṇī*s and *sūtra*s, dedication of merits and burning of incense.

For those who are not yet enlightened certain extra rites are performed to help them achieve liberation. The most important innovation for lay people is their *post mortem* tonsuring and ordination as monks or nuns as part of their preparation for deliverance. If possible this is done before death. Then the lineage chart is transmitted, incorporating the dead into the lineage of the Buddha's family. A sermon is preached on impermanence and the coffin is taken on a circumambulation of the cremation ground, weaving in and out of four gates set at the four points of the compass. The gates symbolise the Four Sights seen by the young Siddhartha as he left the city of Kapilavastu through its four gates. The circumambulation also symbolises the processional route the Buddha's funeral procession took through Kuśinagara. Lastly, the circuitous route is supposed to lose the mind of the deceased so it will not try to find its way back.

Finally, the post-liminal rite of reincorporation involves ten to fifteen days of tea and hot water offerings to the relics, depositing them in a reliquary and 'closing the grave' to prevent the dead spirit returning.

The ritualist/antiritualist dilemma of the Ch'an/Zen funeral is expressed in a verse inscribed on banners at the sides of the cremation site:

> Due to delusion, the three worlds are completed;
> Due to awakening, the ten directions are empty.
> From the outset, there is neither east nor west;
> Where could there be a north and a south?
>
> (Faure 1991: 194)

Zen deals with death by embracing its defilement and transmuting it to purity through its own version of the Buddhist alchemy; as the thirteenth-century Zen master Dogen says:

Simply understand that birth and death is itself *nirvāṇa*, there is nothing to reject as birth and death, nothing to seek as *nirvāṇa*.

(*Shōbōgenzō: Zen Essays by Dōgen*, translated by Thomas Cleary, Honolulu, University of Hawaii Press, 1986: 122)

## NOTES

1. Dickson, J.F. (1875) 'The *Upasampadā-Kammavācā* being the Buddhist manual of the form and manner of ordering of priests and deacons. The Pāli text, with a translation and notes', *Journal of the Royal Asiatic Society of Great Britain and Ireland*, New Series (London), VII, Article I, 1–16.
2. For a discussion of the further consecrations of the Completion stage the reader should consult Snellgrove, D.L. (1987) *Indo-Tibetan Buddhism*, London, Serindia Publications, pp. 243–77; Cozort, D. (1986) *Highest Yoga Tantra*, Ithaca, New York, Snow Lion Publications, pp. 65–133, where he compares the Completion stages of the *Kālacakra* and the *Guhyasamāja tantras*; or Mullin, G.H. (1985) *Selected Works of the Dalai lama I, Bridging the Sūtras and the Tantras* (2nd edn), Ithaca, New York, Snow Lion Publications, pp. 149–86; this contains the First Dalai Lama's commentary on both stages of the *Kālacakra tantra*, with its emphasis on the Completion stage.

## FURTHER READING

*Dīgha Nikāya*: Walshe, Maurice (trans) (1987) *Thus Have I Heard, The Long Discourses of the Buddha*, London, Wisdom Publications.

*Vinaya*: Horner, I.B. (trans) (1966–82) *The Book of the Discipline (Vinaya)* (6 vols) London, The Pali Text Society.

Rhys Davids, T.W. and Oldenberg, H. (1885) *Vinaya Texts* (3 vols), Oxford, Oxford University Press (repr. 1982, Delhi, Motilal).

Akira, H. (trans. P. Groner) (1990) *A History of Indian Buddhism from Śākyamuni to Early Mahāyāna*, Hawaii, University of Hawaii Press.

Atīśa (trans Richard Sherburne, SJ) (1983) *A Lamp for the Path and Commentary*, London, George Allen & Unwin.

Bechert, H. and Gombrich, R. (1984) *The World of Buddhism, Buddhist Monks and Nuns in Society and Culture*, London, Thames and Hudson.
Faure, Bernard (1991) *The Rhetoric of Immediacy: A Cultural Critique of Chan/Zen Buddhism*, Princeton, Princeton University Press.
Gombrich, Richard F. (1971) *Precept and Practice: Traditional Buddhism in the Rural Highlands of Ceylon*, Oxford, Clarendon Press.
Gombrich, Richard F. and Ganath Obeyesekere (1988) *Buddhism Transformed: Religious Change in Sri Lanka*, Princeton, Princeton University Press.
Suzuki, Daisettz T. (n.d.) *The Training of the Zen Buddhist Monk*, New York, Globe Press Books (facsimile of 1934 edn, Kyoto, The Eastern Buddhist Society).
Wayman, Alex (1973) *The Buddhist Tantras: Light on Indo-Tibetan Esotericism*, New York, Samuel Weiser.

# 2. Christianity

*Douglas Davies*

Over the course of nearly two thousand years Christianity has changed from being a small sect of Judaism to a religion with branches in most countries of the world where local customs have influenced Christianity just as, in turn, Christianity has moulded local ways of life. This is especially true as far as movement through different stages of life is concerned because Christianity has brought its own interpretation to periods of birth, adulthood, marriage and death.

As we saw in the Introduction, van Gennep was aware that a rite of passage, as a social event, might not always be timed to correspond exactly with biological maturity or particular psychological states of individuals. This is a significant point, especially if we add to it a religious dimension and say that official church ritual might not always directly reflect the inner state of faith of an individual. In terms of sacraments, for example, a rite may express some theological truth outwardly which, at that particular moment, does not correlate with the inner life of an individual. In some Protestant groups people are not admitted into full membership until they are able to assert that some inner transformation or conversion has taken place. For more Catholic traditions it is enough to assert the ideal of a change through a ritual performance.

## Baptism–confirmation

Baptism is the most fundamental Christian rite of passage. It is one of the additional rituals which Christianity brings to the catalogue of rites performed by humanity in the normal course of human life. By the use of water and in the name of the Holy Trinity a person becomes a member of the Church. The natural substance of water, which is the ordinary medium of washing and cleansing, comes to have several layers of theological meaning when it becomes the water of baptism. The New Testament presents a command of Jesus to the disciples to go and make disciples of all nations 'baptizing them in the name of the Father and of the Son and of the Holy Spirit' (Matt. 28:19–20). John the Baptist appears in all four of the gospels preaching a baptism of repentance for the forgiveness of sins and the coming of God's chosen one. Jesus is then himself baptised by John, an act interpreted by Christians as being not for the forgiveness of sin but to mark the commencement of Jesus's own ministry as the chosen one of God who is to save humankind from their sin and who, in baptism, identifies himself with all people. Paul, one of the most notable early converts to Christianity from Judaism, is himself baptised (Acts 9:18) and is a firm witness to the importance of baptism among early Christians (1 Cor. 1:13ff ).

Just as circumcision had been a mark of membership in the Jewish nation as God's people, so baptism comes to be the defining mark of people being Christian. Many additional meanings were associated with baptismal water. Not only does it remind Christians of the River Jordan in which Jesus was baptised, in his rite of passage into his active public ministry, but it can also represent the Red Sea through which God's people had been delivered from slavery in Egypt. By additional metaphors it stands for the deep waters of death through which Christ was delivered in his resurrection to life, for in baptism the Christian dies to sin and is born again to holiness. Baptismal water can also gain significance in that just as the waters of the womb bring us to our first and natural birth, so the waters of baptism bring us to new birth by the grace of God.

Practically all subsequent Christian groups continued the use of baptism as the basis of membership even though it came to assume different forms and to have varied theological meaning. In the Orthodox, Catholic, Lutheran, and Anglican traditions, the sacramental nature of baptism stresses the divine act of God's grace in forgiveness. Here baptism involves washing from sin, a passage from death to life, a statement of God's covenant established with God's chosen people. This perspective involves what is called sacramental regeneration, which means that the rite itself brings about the desired goal. Some Christians find this interpretation unacceptable and see it as too mechanical and too dependent on the work of the priest and the ritual, and insufficiently related to the heart-felt personal faith of the individual. So, for example, in the Baptist Church, originating in the seventeenth century, and in many evangelical Christian churches, great stress is placed upon the faith of the individual who is to be baptised. For this reason baptism is called believers' baptism and is not administered to babies. In this tradition it is important that individuals should be of an age of discretion – old enough to know what they are doing, aware of the truth of Christianity, and having experienced the forgiving love of God in Christ in their own lives. The service of baptism by immersion allows individuals to acknowledge publicly their faith in Christ before being admitted into the visible body of believers which is the Church. Baptism does not of itself change these individuals in the sense of adding any divine power or grace to them. In terms of rites of passage this self-conscious commitment to Christ, which the adult undertakes in the presence of the congregation of believers, is a rite of incorporation into full membership of the group. Although faith is internal the testimony of faith is external.

During the first five hundred years of its history, church leaders developed the practice of baptism in some quite complex ways. In western Catholic Christianity baptism usually took place at Easter or Pentecost. There was a period, traditionally that of the period of Lent, when candidates were formed into a group called the catechumenate and were taught the Christian faith. They worshipped with the congregation but were not allowed to remain and witness the actual eucharist of the faithful. Before Easter they underwent rituals of exorcism prior to their baptism on Easter Sunday. After baptism in water and in the name of the Holy Trinity they would be vested in white clothes and taken from the baptistry into the body of the church where the bishop laid hands on them and anointed them with oil to receive, and be sealed by, the Holy Spirit. Only then were they fully part of the church and able to share in the eucharist. This scheme follows the process of rites of passage of separation from the old status, period of transition, and rite of incorporation into the new status. By the middle ages, when baptism was increasingly administered to babies, largely because of the theological idea that unbaptised babies would not go to heaven, these rites were compressed and the baby was made a catechumen at the church door before being admitted to be baptised at the font.

In the Eastern Orthodox Church the idea of baptism covered a wider sweep of behaviour than it did in the West, not only focusing on the water rite but also on anointing with oil and the laying on of hands. One major difference emerged between Eastern and Western Christian traditions as time went on and this was that in the West a separation emerged between the use of water and the laying on of hands in the initiation ritual for Christians. In the West the water rite came to be administered by local priests, while the laying on of hands for the conveying of the Holy Spirit took place later and was restricted to the office of the bishop. In the East the priest took over both functions, which meant that the pattern of the earlier tradition was retained to a greater extent than in the West. Eastern rites have also been compressed into shorter periods, but the ritual still retains a phase for the making of a catechumen, involving being breathed on by the priest, blessed with the sign of the cross, exorcisms, the renunciation of evil, and the profession of faith. Baptism proper follows after the water has been blessed and after oil has been blessed and placed on the candidates. Baptism is by total immersion and afterwards the new Christians are dressed in white and receive what is called the sacrament of chrismation, involving anointing numerous parts of the body with chrism and the laying on of hands for the 'seal of the gift of the Holy Spirit'. This sacrament of chrismation is the equivalent of the western rite of confirmation. The distinctive difference is that it follows immediately after the water rite and is part and parcel of the total rite of baptism.

In the West, as is the case in the Church of England, baptism became quite separate from confirmation for two reasons. On the one hand it was due to the fact that priests performed the first and bishops the second (bishops were also far fewer in number than were priests), but on the other there emerged the tradition that baptism was largely performed on babies and confirmation on children from the age of about seven, as preferred by some Catholics, on to the teenage period which became popular in the Anglican Church. This sharp separation of baptism from confirmation runs counter to the earliest Christian tradition where, as we have seen, they formed part of an overall initiation rite. But, an equally important point is that confirmation came to be a distinctive rite, not only gaining the official status as a sacrament in the Roman Catholic Church at the Council of Trent in the late sixteenth century, but also serving in some countries as its own sort of rite of passage.

In many parts of Great Britain, for example, it was customary for younger teenagers to join a confirmation class and to be 'prepared for confirmation'. Separated from ordinary Sunday School children and teachers, they were 'prepared for confirmation' by the parish priest in what was a liminal period, prior to confirmation and incorporation into full church membership at their first communion service. In terms of social history, it appeared odd in Britain when mature adults of thirty or forty years of age presented themselves for confirmation, thus breaking the social pattern of confirmation as a teenage rite of passage into full church membership. This reflects the fact that many babies are no longer baptised and that those who, as adults, come into church membership do so much more in the fashion of early church converts for whom baptism and confirmation as one rite is far more appropriate.

As far as religious studies are concerned it is interesting to see how churches developed theologies to explain changes that occurred in their ritual for non-theological reasons. The split between the water rite and the rite of laying on of hands was closely related to the division of labour between priest and bishop. We have seen how the Eastern Orthodox kept the two rites together within the total process of baptism performed by the priest, while, in the major western churches, the rites were split and attempts were made to develop a theology of confirmation as a distinctive sacrament.

Recent theological debates in Catholic, Anglican, and some other churches, have tried to focus more on baptism as the major rite of passage into membership of the church and to see it as the basis for taking a full part in the eucharist. In the Church of England, for example, unconfirmed children are not permitted to receive the Holy Communion bread and wine despite the fact that they have been baptised. There is a certain lack of theological logic and pastoral insight in this, for some people think that since full participation is part of the very process of developing a knowledge and awareness of God, the children who are prevented from participation are hindered in their spiritual development. From the perspective of rites of passage, as far, for example, as the Church of England is concerned, the status of being a baptised member has shifted from being a post-liminal to being a liminal ritual, with the confirmed status being the post-liminal status of a fully participating member.

## Eucharist

The eucharist itself is sometimes described as a rite of passage in a way that is not entirely appropriate, but it is worth mentioning here as a good example of an occasion that is better described as liminoid than liminal. It is not a rite of passage in the formal sense because it does not conduct a person from one social status to another. What it can do is take people out of their normal everyday and hierarchical form of life and place them for a moment within a context of shared equality together and with God.

One reason why some people make the mistake of seeing the eucharist as a rite of passage is because it does possess something of a threefold pattern. An initial period of confession and absolution from sin separates worshippers from the everyday world of evil and then places them into the transitional phase of worship. While in the liminoid phase they may feel a sense of unity of purpose and fellowship. The theological stress in many modern liturgies on the Holy Spirit as the presence of God at the eucharist reinforces this interpretation of the event, as does the 'sharing of the peace' in an emotional way, as described elsewhere in this chapter. With this sense of unity in mind, the eucharist can be interpreted as involving a liminoid period. Turner described liminoid events in modern society as normally lying outside central political and economic processes as moments when a sense of community is experienced. The Eucharist, Mass, Holy Communion, or Lord's Supper, does very largely lie on the margin of everyday life and takes place in leisure time, and it can provide a sense of community. Not all members of a church may interpret the eucharist in this way, for some people may see the service as a time of private and personal worship rather than as a phase of collective and emotional unity. At the end of the service the people are returned to everyday life in a kind of ritual of reincorporation to normality. In one Anglican form in the *Alternative Service Book*, the service ends with the people praying together, 'Send us out in the power of your Spirit to live and work to your praise and glory'. They are then told by the priest to 'Go in peace to love and serve the Lord'.

This example of the eucharist shows the care needed in using the idea of rites of passage to interpret ceremonies taking place in modern societies, and in particular to draw a distinction between rites which actually alter someone's status and rites that, perhaps, simply alter their mood and quality of relationships with others for a short period. It is also possible to use other ideas to describe these rites in order to draw out different goals attained.

So, for example, we could speak of the eucharist as a *rite of intensification*, when basic beliefs and sentiments are focused upon and experienced anew. Many repetitive rites of a society foster such an intensification, as in the case of renewal of baptismal or ordination vows. Another way of talking of such ceremonies is to see them as 'accessive' rites, providing occasions when particular beliefs are made explicit through the arousal of particular moods. The main distinction between rites of passage and rites of intensification is that most people undergo a rite of passage only once, as in confirmation, but they repeatedly experience accessive rites of intensification such as the eucharist.

Periodic festivals celebrating Christmas, harvest, birthdays, and anniversaries are all examples of repetitive rites that are not rites of passage (except for some birthdays when the age of majority is attained) but which may well include a liminoid sense of unity and oneness.

## Thanksgiving, blessing, and naming

Those Protestant churches where baptism takes place in adult life or where parents choose not to have their children baptised as infants, often undertake a service of thanksgiving for the child. A good example may be found in the Church of England's new *Alternative Service Book* (1980), which included a special service of Thanksgiving for the Birth of a Child. This Anglican service is interesting as far as religious studies are concerned because it has undergone a series of changes indicating shifts in theological emphasis and in social conditions. From a brief historical perspective we can see the service change, starting from a medieval service for the 'Purification of Women' after childbirth (in the 1549 Prayer Book). This ritual for the purification of mothers focuses more on the woman than on the child and was a thanksgiving for her safety during childbirth. In England this took place about a month after the baby was born; in one medieval rite she was met by the priest at the church door, sprinkled with holy water, and then led into church. In the 1552

Prayer Book the service is called 'The Thanksgiving of Women after Childbirth commonly called The Churching of Women'. By the time of the *Alternative Service Book*, the service has become one of thanksgiving for the birth of a child.

In terms of rites of passage, a switch has occurred from a focus on the woman and her return to ordinary social life to that of the child and thanksgiving for its birth. It is likely that the older rite for the Purification of Women readmitted them to normal social activity after the birth of a child, for pregnancy has often been viewed as a liminal period in which the woman, especially if she was childless, moved into the status of motherhood from that of simply being a wife.

Children are themselves blessed and sometimes given their Christian name at these services of thanksgiving, as they are in the rite of baptism. Such name-giving is an important moment, marking as it does the fact that the child is given a social identity of its own. Babies are often dressed in special white robes or dresses for thanksgiving or baptism services. Such 'christening robes' continue to express the traditional Christian practice of initiates being dressed in white at their baptism to symbolise the freedom from sin brought about through the baptismal washing.

## Marriage

Being a major life event in terms of changed social status marriage would be expected to involve rites of passage. In this case the passage is from a variety of unmarried states to the one married state. This is obviously the case in that prior to the marriage individuals may be single, divorced, or bereaved as widows or widowers. After marriage they are husbands or wives.

Most present-day Christian churches practise marriage rites and the image of, for example, the Church of England's marriage service, with bells, organ, and vicar, all set within an ancient building, has become an established part of British cultural life. But Christian churches have not always conducted marriages and, compared with baptism, the eucharist, and death rites, marriage is a slightly relative newcomer to Christian ritual as is shown below. For the moment we stay with present practice to interpret marriage in terms of rites of passage.

The pre-liminal phase involves separation from purely single and unattached life. In Britain this is an informal and personal period but does involve a change when young men and young women no longer fill their leisure time in the company of a group of same-sex people. A couple going out together on a regular basis is the informal mark of a pre-liminal phase which is formally marked with the giving of an engagement ring.

The engagement is the liminal period when the couple are no longer single and unattached but neither are they formally married. In the Church of England, as the state church of England, their transitional status is expressed in the reading of the banns, which takes place over three separate weeks preceding the marriage in the parish churches where the individuals live. Only with the marriage ceremony, either in a church or else in a civil registry office, does the liminal phase end and the post-liminal status of married life begin. Sometimes there is an engagement party, but there is nearly always a formal social celebration to mark the marriage.

As far as the wedding ceremony, especially in church, is concerned the ritual very interestingly expresses the change in status that now occurs. The bride and groom are formally separated for a day before the wedding. They will probably celebrate with their single-sex friends in a stag-night or hen-party a day or so before the wedding. He is not supposed to see her on the wedding day, nor even see her wedding dress until she appears in church. He will have gone there with his best-man and entered in an unceremonious way. The bride enters accompanied by her father who is, traditionally, said to 'give her away'. The bride's family and friends sit on one side of the church and the groom's family and friends on the other.

Generally speaking there are two dimensions to wedding rites; on the one hand there is a legal ceremony in which promises are made between bride and groom, and on the other, a religious blessing of the couple with prayers for their future life. In eastern and western Christendom these elements are stressed in quite different ways.

In western Catholic and Protestant Christianity the marriage rite is actually performed by bride and groom rather than by the priest. They are the heart of their own rite of passage into marriage as is clearly shown in, for example, the Anglican rite where the bride says, 'I . . . take thee . . . to my wedded husband', and also, when the man says 'With this ring I thee wed, with my body I thee honour, and with all my worldly goods I thee endow'. The priest pronounces that they are man and wife only because they have made each other so. The prayers that follow bless them as husband and wife but do not make them husband and wife.

In Eastern Orthodox Christianity there is also a betrothal of each to each, as a form of natural human bond, but this is then taken up into a sacramental rite in which the priest crowns the husband and the wife as a central feature of the wedding. This expresses the hierarchy of the Holy Trinity extended into that of husband and wife. They share in drinking wine together as a symbolic expression of their unity, and they go in procession within the church to express the unity they possess within the mystical fellowship of Christ which cannot be broken, even by death. This contrasts sharply with the western tradition and its stress upon the contractual nature of marriage which exists 'till death us do part'.

We have already mentioned that marriage was a relatively late ritual to be taken up by the Christian churches. In their early history churches had prayers for blessing those who had married by the normal rules of their society, but it was only in the eleventh century in the West that the church became a central and dominant focus for marriage for almost the next thousand years. Civil marriage in Britain was firmly established only by the Marriage Act, passed by Parliament in 1836. By the late 1980s, just about half of all wedding ceremonies took place in church and half in a registry office. Slightly more detail shows that nearly seventy per cent of all first marriages took place in churches of some denomination but, by contrast, some seventy-six per cent of all second marriages, which involve divorced people, took the form of civil marriages. This shows a continued preference for the church form of ceremony for the first wedding. Even some of those whose second marriages take place in registry offices then go to church for a service of blessing.

Such a service of blessing a marriage is, as we have seen from the history of marriage rites, quite logical given the nature of marriage in European culture, where the first major focus is on the partners marrying each other before the Church pronounces a blessing on the union. Remarriage brings to an end the period as a bereaved or divorced person, two statuses that need to be considered in their own right.

## Divorce

Divorce is a problem because churches argue that marriage is for life. So, for example, in the traditional wedding service of the Church of England both bride and groom are asked if they will have the other as their marriage partner to love, honour and keep in sickness and in health, 'so long as you both shall live'. Then, in the actual statement where each one takes the other as a spouse the fact of death is clearly mentioned, as in the words the man says to the woman:

> I . . . take thee . . . to my wedded wife,
> to have and to hold from this day forward
> for better for worse, for richer for poorer,
> in sickness and in health, to love and to cherish
> till death us do part, according to God's holy ordinance . . .

The woman then makes a very similar statement to the man. In both statements marriage is assumed to be for the whole of their earthly life and for no longer. For many reasons the union between husband and wife does not always last this long. Traditional Catholic teaching has argued that once a real marriage union exists it cannot be dissolved by any human power. This line of thinking leads to attempts at showing that no proper and full marriage existed between people. The Orthodox tradition, even though it has a high idea of marriage as a relationship in Christ that transcends death, has accepted the idea that a marriage can die and a divorce be granted. The Protestant and Reformed tradition has stressed that marriage ought not to be dissolved, but has accepted divorce for particular reasons, usually those of immorality.

The Church of England, representing within itself elements both of Catholic and Reformed traditions, has generally accepted the reality of divorce but has largely objected to the remarriage of divorced people in church while the divorced partner is still alive. This explains why some clergy are prepared to hold a service of blessing on a second marriage that has already taken place according to a civil rite. Divorce is an increasingly common status in modern society and comes about through legal procedures and not through religious rites. The status of being divorced has no formal rites of passage associated with it.

## Bereavement

In some respects bereavement resembles divorce while in others it differs significantly. Bereavement begins for most people with the funeral of the deceased; thereafter the surviving spouse is a widow or a widower, and children are without father or mother but do not have a distinct status because of that unless they become orphans at the loss of both parents.

In some Christian cultures, especially Orthodox and Catholic ones where church rites have become intimately associated with the traditional practices of a people, there are formal celebrations of anniversaries of the death which help locate the widow as a member of the community. But in many modern western societies fixed periods of mourning are not widely practised and there is no settled convention as to the identity and status of widows and widowers. In terms of rites of passage, some bereaved people seem to be in an extended period of liminality with no settled position in society. This is the case because, for example, a widow may remain a widow or may marry again. The status of widowhood is a slightly variable one, and in this it resembles divorce. Sometimes divorced and bereaved people speak in similar ways about their sense of identity as one which is difficult for other people to handle. A central issue lies in the fact that in many modern societies married couples engage in leisure activity together along with many other couples. Once a person ceases to be one of a couple they fit less easily into the leisure world of social life. But human societies are adaptable and some people join groups or clubs for the divorced or widowed which help provide an arena for leisure.

Similarly, some individuals carry out a kind of private rite of passage which is significant for them. A bereaved woman might, for example, decide to remove her wedding ring or to wear it on a different finger from that on which the ring was placed at her wedding. In the same way, a divorced person might decide to bury or otherwise dispose of the wedding ring as a sign that the old relationship was now finished.

These examples throw light on the power of firmly established rites of passage to help guide individuals in their ordinary life. When human behaviour changes fairly rapidly a gap emerges between tradition and the way present life functions, a gap that is problematic for many people. It is likely that new customs may emerge to furnish rites of passage for new situations.

## Marrying forever: eternal rites of passage?

If some people are glad to have divorce as a legal act that serves as a rite of passage into the single state, some others do not even wish to accept the death of a spouse as the end of their relationship. In the broad western Christian tradition of theology death ends marriage. A saying of Jesus in Mark's gospel is often taken to focus the issue:

> When they rise from the dead they neither marry nor are given in marriage but are like angels in heaven.
>
> (Mark 12:25)

In some popular Christian views the idea of life after death has been extended to embrace the idea that husbands and wives, indeed whole families, will be together in heaven. In terms of formal doctrine, one religious movement has taken this idea as central to its view of life and possesses distinct rites of passage to express it. The group is that of the Church of Jesus Christ of Latter-day Saints, commonly called the Mormon Church.

This Church believes that through the power of the priesthood, restored to mankind through the founding prophet, Joseph Smith, men and women may be sealed together forever. Marriages performed in ordinary Mormon churches or in registry offices are 'for time' and life in this world only, but marriages sealed in one of the Mormon Temples are also 'for eternity'. In terms of rites of passage and of Mormon thought, a Temple marriage brings the mark of eternity to bear upon what otherwise belongs only to time. Couples sealed in the Temple will remain together for all eternity and may also have their children sealed to them in a similar Temple ritual. In fact, the Church of Jesus Christ of Latter-day Saints sees the extended family as the fundamental basis of eternal life and of salvation, so much so that, through another rite of passage, living family members are baptised on behalf of dead family members who did not know about Mormon doctrine and its way of life. This 'baptism for the dead' offers a means of incorporating ancestors into the Mormon family for eternity.

These particular Mormon rites are interesting in that they are vicarious, undertaken on behalf of someone else. Many Mormon rites can be performed in this vicarious way, which explains how Mormons interpret the text from Mark's gospel which has already been quoted, saying that there is no marriage in heaven. This text might, initially, seem quite contradictory to Mormon ideas of marriage as the basic unit of celestial existence. Mormons agree that there is indeed no marriage in heaven, but in the sense that there are no marriage rites performed in heaven. In order to be in a married state in the eternal world one needs to have been married through the power of the priesthood within a Latter-day Saint Temple on earth, either personally or vicariously.

## Death

We have already considered changes in status for those who are bereaved. But, for Christian theology, death primarily focuses on the change of status of the person who has died. As the twentieth century has proceeded, funerary customs have changed quite significantly in many countries and the process still goes on, which means that any description of funerary rites must acknowledge the change that is still occurring. The major change in Britain, and in some parts of Europe, lies in the rise of cremation, and crematoria as the place where the body meets its end, and also in the rise of funeral homes as places where the body is kept rather than in the domestic setting of the house of the deceased.

From the earliest days of the religion Christians have linked the death and funerals of believers with the death and resurrection of Christ. The ritual of the last rites in the Catholic tradition involved confession of sin, absolution by the priest, anointing with oil, and communion. The idea was to prepare the dying for the journey to God which was about to follow; the communion part of the rite was even called the *viaticum*, a Latin term for the provisions for a journey.

After death came the preparation of the body for burial, followed in most church traditions by a service marking the movement of the dead from the realm of the living. This brief ritual takes place on the day of the funeral at the home of the deceased, at a special funeral home where the dead person has been kept, or else at the reception of the dead body into the church the night before the funeral.

On the day of the funeral this short service precedes the journey which leads the body away from its human home to the church, to the cemetery, or to the crematorium, where the main service takes place. There is variation here, since sometimes a church service precedes a service at the crematorium while at others there is no service at church, and yet in other circumstances the main service is at church with very little ritual performed at the crematorium.

Wherever the major rite occurs it serves as a liminal period where the dead body stands between the world of human social life and that of its final eternal destiny. The Christian doctrine of the resurrection of Jesus deeply influences the funeral service because the dead are buried or cremated in the hope of a future life brought about through a divine act of resurrection. Just as Jesus was raised from the dead so the dead Christian will be brought to a new existence through the creative power of God. God is thanked for the life that the person led, the congregation is reminded of the mortal nature of human life and all are encouraged to lead their own earthly lives in the light of this knowledge. The dead person is then given back to the earth, or to the fire, on the understanding that we come from the natural elements and to them we return until God's new creation, symbolised in the resurrection of Jesus.

The service ends with the dead being given a new status, incorporated into the eternal world. No longer part of the living world the dead now take their place among the Communion of Saints in the care of God. This shift of status is associated with what happens to the mortal remains. The shift from living status to the status of being dead takes place either when the body is buried in a grave or else when the body is burned and the ashes buried or scattered in some sacred or significant place.

This picture of a rite of separation in the first service at home, a rite of transition in the major service, and a rite of incorporation into the other world through burial of remains is, however, slightly too simple, for the reason that many contemporary Christians place greater significance on the immortality of the soul than on the resurrection of the body. For such people the soul is believed to leave the body at death and go into the nearer presence of God; even so the body continues to represent something of the identity of the deceased and its final burial or cremation indicates the end of the public life of that person in this world. Even so, in terms of Christian theology the idea of a body, or more properly, of a resurrection-body, has played an important part in the idea of continuity of identity between a person in this earthly life and the same person in heaven. The nature of the relation between the two produced some interesting speculation, including St Augustine's belief that in the resurrection God would give perfect bodies to those who had some deficiency in their earthly body, just as he would ensure that those who died as babies would be resurrected full grown:

> I say they shall not rise with that littleness of body in which they died, but that the sudden and strange power of God shall give them a stature of full growth.
>
> (*City of God*, Book 22, cap. 14)

Ideas about the body and the soul run parallel in much practical Christian thought with several consequences. In the Catholic tradition the liturgy for the dead refers to the journey the soul undertakes as it moves to God and is welcomed by the saints. Sometimes a special Requiem Mass is said for the dead as a means of benefiting them in the after-life through the offering of the Mass and the prayers of the church. The funeral service is sometimes set within the context of a Requiem Mass, and such masses are also used on the occasion of anniversaries of death. The Protestant tradition has been far less ready to talk about and assume any knowledge of what awaits any particular individual; for this reason the prayers for the dead which are central to the Catholic tradition are largely missing among Protestants.

## Against cremation

While many churches of the Protestant tradition came to accept cremation relatively early in the twentieth century, the Roman Catholic Church did so only in the 1960s, while the Orthodox Churches have continued their opposition to the practice. The Orthodox example is interesting for it shows perhaps the most traditional of ancient Christian approaches to death, and also enshrines a fundamental commitment to the resurrection of Christ as a dominant aspect of its theology and liturgy. The forms of service differ depending upon whether the dead is a child, layperson, or priest. The general pattern follows the threefold distinction between service at the home, in church, and at the grave. The overall scheme is that of a journeying procession. One prayer that is sung in each phase is an ancient prayer for the dead which addresses God as 'God of spirits and of all flesh, who has trampled down death and overthrown the devil and given life to the world'. This reflects the Christian sense of death as the triumph of God over evil through Christ and his resurrection.

The coffin is placed in the church in such a way that the face of the dead looks towards the altar; the coffin is normally open. The hymns and scriptures sung are the same as for Holy Saturday, the day before Easter Sunday, symbolically expressing the fact that this day is the day of awaiting the resurrection. In terms of rites of passage the funeral day is truly a liminal period between the old life of this world and the life of the world to come. A further section of the service reminds the living of the mixed nature of life where joys and sorrows intermingle; then the soul of the individual is addressed and told that a place of rest awaits it. Finally, the congregation gives the kiss of peace to the corpse to symbolise that it is still part of the total fellowship of the church in Christ.

At the grave earth is placed on the coffin in the form of a cross and the grave blessed to receive the body, then all are dismissed. At this final moment all sing a prayer enshrining the Orthodox idea of 'memory eternal': in Orthodox theology this refers to a belief that it is Jesus who keeps the dead alive in the memory of God.

In Mediterranean village contexts of Greek Orthodox life, the dead are not simply left in the grave forever. It has been traditional for the bones of the dead to be removed from the grave between three and five years after the burial and to be placed in the village ossuary. During this period it is customary for women from the village who have been bereaved to visit the graves where they continue a kind of relationship with the dead. For such women the total rite of passage of death takes the shape of a rite of separation, marked by the total funeral ending in burial, then a very long liminal period during which the body of the dead decays, and when they increasingly come to accept the death in terms of their own psychology, then finally as the bones are removed from the earth and incorporated into the village ossuary the women fully enter into their identity as a widow. Against that style of burial rite it is quite understandable why Orthodox religion objects to cremation, even in terms of the practical processes of grief and accommodation to the single life. More important still, however, is the theological stress placed upon the final resurrection of Christ and on the part played by that belief in many other parts of Orthodox thinking and practice.

## Ordination

Ordination is one rite of passage that has affected a small but significant group of people within Christendom for many centuries. From the earliest period of the Christian Church certain individuals were set apart to lead the believing community. By about the fourth century there is a discernible pattern of bishops, priests, and deacons, each having a recognisable function, especially in worship. Bishops and priests were set apart by the laying on of hands, a rite that continues to this day. Other minor orders in the early church period were those of doorkeeper, reader, exorcist, and acolyte, but they have ceased to be of widespread significance in later periods.

### ORDINATION AND PRIESTHOOD

As church traditions developed and diverged so did the more detailed nature of ordination; even so the pattern of bishop, deacon, and priest was retained in Orthodox, Catholic, Anglican, and Lutheran traditions, even when their precise theological significance was altered. Many Protestant churches largely abandoned this threefold order and have focused on a non-priestly minister of the word as a central figure who tends to share leadership along with a group of non-ordained laypeople.

In contemporary life the rite of passage of ordination follows an identifiable pattern. The first period is one of separation from a purely lay status through a process of selection and choice on the part of the church. It is marked by the distinct identity of ordinand, one who has been selected and is now in training for the sacred ministry of the church. This period will often take three or so years and may be longer. On the one hand it is a time of education in theology, church history, and pastoral matters but, on the other, it is also a time of spiritual formation and development in prayer and worship.

Even this period of training is not the end of the process of preparation, which is taken a step further when the individual is made a deacon for a period, of perhaps a year, before actually being ordained priest. Being made deacon marks the beginning of the fully liminal period, for in many respects the deacon represents the status of being between laity and priesthood; although dressed like priests, deacons may not celebrate the eucharist.

In many traditions this long period of training and diaconate is symbolised and comes to an end in a retreat prior to the actual ordination to the priesthood, when liminality ends and the individual is incorporated into the status and office of priest. The ordination service itself throws into sharp focus the fact that the individual's life is now dedicated to the service of God and God's people. The tasks of ministry are spelled out and objects appropriate to that ministry are given. In some traditions this involves a copy of the holy scriptures, priestly vestments, and eucharistic vessels. It is made clear that the dedication and promises involved are lifelong. This was traditionally reinforced for the threefold order in the Catholic Church and in the case of bishops in the Orthodox Church by admitting only single men to these offices, indicating a kind of marriage to the office of ministry.

## Ministry and priesthood of all believers

There is a major difference between the idea of priesthood in the Orthodox, Catholic, and some strands of the Anglican traditions on the one hand, and in the Protestant Reformed traditions on the other. The former see priesthood as affecting an individual for life, and in some traditions even imprinting an indelible priestly character upon the very being of the individual concerned. This tradition also stresses sacrifice and mediation between humanity and God as a major function of the priest – the priest sacrifices on behalf of, and to mediate for, others. From the period of reform initiated by Martin

Luther in the early sixteenth century, the Protestant tradition repudiated these dimensions and developed the doctrine of the priesthood of all believers by right of their baptism. All God's people, it is argued, are priests in the sense that they represent themselves before God and have no need of any sacrifice because Christ sacrificed himself and is the great high priest of all Christians. For the purpose of good church organisation some believers are chosen to exercise their priesthood as a ministry for a particular church community. This representative function of priesthood may only last for a particular period in a particular place, and the office focuses on the preaching and teaching of the word of God in Holy Scripture.

If many Protestant churches developed their ministry through the doctrine of the priesthood of all believers in such a way that a few people served as ministers for many, one western religious movement, that of the Church of Jesus Christ of Latter-day Saints, often called the Mormon Church, has popularised priesthood in the opposite direction. All Mormon males hold an office, first within the Aaronic Priesthood with its three grades of deacon, teacher, and priest, which extend from the twelfth to the nineteenth year of age, and secondly within the Melchizedek Priesthood, composed of all worthy males from their early twenties onward. Their duties vary depending upon grade but all are ordained for their tasks and help form a firm church organisation. Ordination is usually by the laying on of hands with prayer, and is one means of impressing young people with the seriousness of their religion and encouraging in them a sense of identity as part of a greater system of priesthood, one that is ultimately shared by God in the Mormon understanding of reality. Many rites of passage are experienced by Mormons as they move from one grade of priesthood to another and this encourages a sense of development and progression throughout life, something that is in accord with the Mormon idea of eternity as an ever-developing scheme of reality.

## Religious orders

From relatively early times some Christians have felt called to serve God by living in religious communities as monks and nuns. A distinctive feature of this way of life is celibacy where people remain single to devote themselves to a life of prayer and of various kinds of service to the world. Entry into religious orders such as the black-robed Benedictines, whose history extends from the sixth century, or the Franciscans and Dominicans, which originated in the thirteenth century, usually involves very distinct rites of passage. As a postulant, candidates enter a phase of separation from the world at large, often of several months' duration. If successful they become a novice in a probationary period under the guidance of a senior member of the order. This liminal period is usually symbolised by being clothed in the distinctive robes of the order while not having been fully admitted to it. If finally successful, candidates are incorporated as full members of the order in a ritual that resembles a marriage, which explains why nuns are sometimes seen as brides of Christ and wear a wedding ring. In addition to the vow of chastity, vows of poverty and obedience are also taken.

## Fellowship and unity

But for ordinary Christians such a separate existence is not possible and may not even be viewed as desirable. What is important in theological terms is that Christians have a sense of belonging together in a community of believers as the people of God. Sometimes this ideal is simply stated, but at other times it becomes a much more tangible awareness.

On a small scale, a sense of unity and fellowship can be reproduced for periods of Christian mission and worship, especially during periods of religious revivalism such as occurred, for example, in South Wales in 1904. Many village communities, both industrial and rural, experienced periods when the power of God seemed to transform individuals. People repented of their sins in public worship and were caught up in hymn-singing as they felt themselves to be born again as new people.

It is often the case that music and singing serve to integrate and unite people in liminoid moments. Even the example of the 1991 World Cup in the sporting realm of football demonstrated the power of song, in this case through the operatic theme sung by the Italian tenor, Luciano Pavarotti.

## *Koinonia* and *communitas*

One interesting biblical example of the sense of *communitas* can be found in the Acts of the Apostles (2:42–47) where, for a short period after the day of Pentecost, the early Christians are described as sharing in fellowship with the apostles and with each other as they sold their goods, and worshipped and ate together. The divisions of society, not only in terms of hierarchy, but also the distinction between Jew and gentile, were to be overcome in the early life of the emerging Christian Church, so well attested in the Acts of the Apostles. This suggests that the Greek word for fellowship and for having things in common, *koinonia*, reflects Turner's idea of community and oneness expressed in his term *communitas*. But such moments as these do not last. As time goes on, the very human tendency towards organised and hierarchical forms of life re-establishes itself, so much so that, in the First Letter to the Christians at Corinth, Christians need to be reminded of their status as one with another and with Christ and to be called to live accordingly (1 Cor. 1:10ff).

Victor Turner appreciated the fragile quality of *communitas*, just as many Christians recognise the fact that a sense of unity and love which is sometimes experienced in worship, religious gatherings, conferences, or missions does not often last for long. As the introductory chapter shows, Turner not only interpreted human life in society as a kind of pendulum swing from organised hierarchy into *communitas* and back again, but also defined several types of *communitas* to cover the responses people make to these switches in experience. His scheme is quite useful when interpreting aspects of Christian ritual and theology.

One interesting historical example of spontaneous *communitas* occurred in the Moravian Church gathered on the estates of Count Zinzendorf at Herrnhut in Germany in 1727. The congregation, coming to church on 13 August, felt a sense of unity and love that was quite overpowering. After the service the Count sent food to some of the homes of church members and they ate what came to be called a Love Feast together in this atmosphere of unity. Subsequent Moravian communities have held love feasts to celebrate many kinds of church activities, and in these that historical moment of spontaneous *communitas* is reflected in the normative style of *communitas* contained in the formal nature of a church service.

Another form of community is expressed in many services of mainstream Christian churches today, where it has become customary for there to be a moment when the 'peace is passed' at the eucharist. This is a traditional liturgical act which can be conducted in a strictly formal way. In some churches, however, especially those influenced by the Charismatic Movement of a more enthusiastic and emotionally explicit style of religion, this period introduces a much less formal moment when people wander around the church hugging or otherwise greeting each other. This could be interpreted as a form of *communitas* which sometimes demonstrates a spontaneous character and at others a level of intensity that merely hints at the possibility of spontaneity.

## Identity and authenticity

The relationship between a stated theological ideal and an actual personal experience of the truth enshrined in it is complex within Christianity. In many Protestant traditions a person comes to a full sense of identity after religious conversion or, as in the case with some renewal movements associated with charismatic groups, when they have a new kind of experience enabling them to speak in tongues or heal other people. It is not easy to determine if and when people will undergo such transformations so that formal rites of passage do not usually exist in these groups, but the experience itself can be a kind of rite of passage. For it is when people first speak in tongues or receive a vision in a communal context that they are, as it were, accorded recognition as being part of the acceptable inner circle of the faithful.

In terms of Christian thinking, the relationship between a formal ritual status and the inner life of a person is of vital importance. Individuals are called to live their lives in a heart-felt and sincere way and not simply to obey official rules attached to a social status. In the world of everyday life husbands and wives must love each other and not simply follow rules for married people, just as leaders in the church must have an inner sense of identity with their calling rather than simply follow rules attached to their social status.

This is one reason why it is important to think of self-identity as something a person grows into. Individuals come to a deep awareness of their place in the world through their life experience, through what can be called a sense of embodiment. Our bodies and our life experiences are not simply intellectual or rational things, they are also deeply emotional, and this is why the idea of embodiment is important: it is as thinking and feeling bodies that we live, change and enter fully into ourselves as we express ourselves to others. It is as embodied individuals that we undergo rites of passage. If we speak about people only in terms of the roles they have in life or, for example, of the parts they play in social dramas, then we get the idea that humans are actors who wear their costume and cosmetics only on the outsides of their lives. The idea of roles played in life is useful but it has its limits. Excessive stress on roles and role-models easily leads to a superficial understanding of people and needs to be kept firmly in place through the perspective of embodiment. In rites of passage many of the symbols used touch the experience of people in an emotional way and can enter quite deeply into what we might call their mood memory.

So it is that identity involves depth of emotion in embodiment as well as including roles that are learned in more formal ways. The links between status and growing awareness of identity may be quite complex. In some churches, such as the Church of England where baptism often takes place while people are still babies, Christian status comes long before any personal sense of identity as a follower of Christ. In that case, a sense of identity grows with time as a person enters into the status that has already been given in baptism. In a similar way people are formally given the status of husband and wife on the day of their marriage but it may take time for them to grow into their own sense of identity as married partners. Conversely, they may already have lived together in practical terms as husband and wife some time before they undertake the ritual of marriage.

## Conclusion

In this chapter we have shown how Christianity marks certain changes in social status and actually initiates changed identity in others. We have also distinguished between liminal and liminoid phases in ritual, and have shown how certain rites bring about new changes while other rites intensify changes that have already been established. In conclusion it is worth stressing the important fact that changed social statuses are linked to changing self-identity in complex processes that depend much upon the individual and, in terms of Christian theology, also upon the relationship between the creative nature of God and the faith of individuals.

## FURTHER READING

Augustine, St (1945) *City of God*, London, Dent.
Campbell, V.C. (1987) *A Dictionary of Pastoral Care*, London, Society for Promoting Christian Knowledge (SPCK).
Davies, D.J. (1990) *Cremation Today and Tomorrow*, Nottingham, GROW–Alcuin Books.
Davies, J.G. (1986) *A New Dictionary of Liturgy and Worship*, London, SCM Press.
Stevenson, K.W. (1982) *Nuptial Blessings: A Study of Christian Marriage Rites*, London, Alcuin Club.

# 3. Hinduism

*Gavin Flood*

Recent scholarly debates about the nature of ritual have tended to regard it either as primarily expressive of symbolic systems, concerned with communication between ritual actors, or as primarily functional or pragmatic, concerned with the bringing about of specific goals.[1] That is, ritual has been regarded either as a way in which humans 'speak' with each other within a community and through the generations, and with putative transhuman entities as well, or as a kind of magical technology which brings about effects desired by an individual or group. Because of the varieties of ritual theories, particularly within anthropology, perhaps the most fruitful way of arriving at an understanding of Hindu rites of passage is to begin with an indigenous, Hindu classification of its own ritual systems. Hinduism has understood ritual in terms of both communication and pragmatism, and even, by some ritualists, as action for its own sake with no other purpose. As Piatigorsky has observed, in examining Indian religion we are examining something which has already examined itself and developed terms for its own self-description.[2] Such indigenous systems of classification are of vital importance in understanding Hindu rites of passage.

The authoritative sources for Hindu rites of passage are the secondary revelation, or *smṛti* texts (see 'Hinduism' in *Sacred Writings* in this series). These, based on the primary revelation of the Veda (Manu 2.6–7), are the group of writings subsumed under the general category of *Kalpa sūtra*s or ritual manuals. These texts, composed about the sixth century BCE, comprise three categories: the *Śrauta sūtra*s, concerned with explaining the sacrificial procedures of the older *Brāhmaṇa*s; the *Dharma sūtra*s, concerned with correct human conduct; and the *Gṛhya sūtra*s, concerned with domestic religious observances. It is this latter category of texts which is mainly concerned with the performance of rites of passage, though the *Dharma sūtras* and *śāstras* (authoritative treatises) also contain accounts of these rites. In the *Gṛhya sūtras* and in Manu we find the rites of passage classed as a 'bodily rite' (*śarīra-saṃskāra*), in contrast to daily and seasonal rites, a distinction which is maintained in the *Dharma śāstras*. These texts are not, however, the only sources, there being regional, oral traditions (*laukika*) which have contributed to the development of rites of passage. Thus, high caste rites of passage in any particular region of India will be a fusion of śāstric and folk elements.

The *smṛti* literature divides ritual into three classes: obligatory, daily rites (*nitya-karman*), occasional rites (*naimittika-karman*) and rites for a desired object or purpose (*kāmya-karman*) (ritual in the pragmatic sense mentioned above). Rites of passage fall within the second category of rituals 'occasioned by a special occurrence' (*Āpastamba Gṛhya-sūtra* 1.1.11). They are of central importance in constructing 'Hindu' identity within the overriding brahmanical culture which has moulded Hindu traditions and maintained the continuity of those traditions.

## *Saṃskāra* and *Dharma*

A fundamental distinction can be made within Indian religions between soteriology and worldly life.[3] This distinction is explicit in philosophical traditions, such as Advaita Vedānta, which distinguished between liberating knowledge of the absolute and ritual action, and in the social institutions of the world-renouncer and the householder. While the renouncer's final goal is liberation (*mokṣa*), the householder is concerned with daily ritual activity. Rites of passage are entirely within the realm of the householder's life and are nothing to do with the Hindu soteriology of freedom from the cycle of reincarnation which the renouncer is seeking (except in so far as only twice-born males in orthodox Hinduism can generally become renouncers). Hindu rites of passage are concerned with the transition between different phases in the life of the householder and do not include the rite of renunciation or the various sectarian initiations which may be regarded as liberating (see below). Although Manu says that the performance of *dharma*, which would include rites of passage, does lead to happiness after death (Manu 2.9), this is not salvation, which is beyond social laws and cannot be attained through rites concerned with social transformation.

The Sanskrit term used for rites of passage is *saṃskāra*, implying something which is 'put together' or 'constructed' (from *saṃ* 'together' plus *kāra* from the root *kṛ* 'to make'). The term is appropriate and reflects the early Hindu perception that rites of passage, or transformative rites, moulded or helped construct social identities. The importance of the *saṃskāra*s in this process cannot be overestimated. They are the link between the higher order laws of the transpersonal *dharma*, and the personal reality of the high caste householder, moulding his or her life to the culture and community to which he or she belongs. Through the *saṃskāra*s people's social role and even, to some extent, ontological status, are defined, and through the *saṃskāra* they are given access to the resources within the tradition which were previously closed to them. Through the *saṃskāra* the initiate enters into a new field of activity and awareness, a new realm or state.

The *saṃskāra*s are transformative processes linking different states. The distinction between 'state' and 'process' indicates that 'society' (identified with 'state') is a hierarchical structure of relations, while the rite of passage is an interstructural situation between social positions; it is 'period of margin or liminality' (see Introduction, pp. 3–4 above). The liminal condition characteristic of rites of passage functions to reinforce social institutions: liminality is legitimised by the society and in turn legitimises the social structure. Hence rather than 'rites of passage', Bourdieu refers to them as 'rites of institution'.[4] The Hindu *saṃskāra*s are thus rites of institution in that they serve to maintain social order.

Hindu society has developed as a hierarchy which, for any one person, has been experienced as a series of 'states' connected by liminal periods or processes. This society has developed over the centuries as a complex structure in which social relations have been delineated in terms of purity (*śuddha*) and impurity (*aśuddha*), auspiciousness (*śubha*) and inauspiciousness (*aśubha*).[5] Concern for the network of social relations has been one of the main features, if not the main feature, of *dharma*, a complex term which encompasses social duties and responsibilities. In the *saṃskāra*s we can see the practical application of *dharma*, specifically of the *varṇāśrama-dharma*, duty with regard to one's class/caste (*varṇa*) and stage of life (*āśrama*) (see 'Hinduism' in *Making Moral Decisions* in this series).

For the Hindu householder (the majority of Hindus), the maintaining of *dharma* ensures a morally upright life. Madan cites the example of the Kashmiri Brahmans or Pandits, whose life is governed by *dharma*, which they understand as '*bhaṭṭil*': the Bhaṭṭa's or Kashmiri Brahman's life-style, largely concerned with domesticity and the householder's purposes of life (*artha*). This is so central to their world-view and their lives, that it alone is sufficient reason for doing anything in a particular way. Madan writes: 'When children . . . and even curious adults ask of those who might know why something should be done in a particular way, or done at all, the Pandit answer usually is: "it is *bhaṭṭil*, it is our way of life"' (Madan 1987: 30).

Rites of passage are *dharma* or *bhaṭṭil* in action. They are the expression of *dharma* in time; the way in which *dharma* works through a person's life, marking the exit from one dharmically determined social state and the entry to another. Rites of passage are therefore connected with ethics in so far as the actors in a ritual, in R.A. Rappaport's words, 'accept, and indicate to themselves and to others that they accept, the order encoded in that ritual'.[6] Morality is, as Rappaport points out, 'intrinsic to ritual' in that through accepting the constraints of the ritual a participant is accepting the moral constraints of the tradition. In performing the *saṃskāra*s Hindus are subjecting themselves to the higher power of *dharma* and allowing themselves to be moulded by that higher force.

The power of *dharma* is expressed through ritual in the body. Rites of passage are focused on the body and its transformations over time, leading through the process of maturation to eventual death. In being centred on the body, the Hindu rites of passage are an expression in the human, material world of the transpersonal, cosmic *dharma* which itself is eternal (*sanātana*) (see 'Hinduism' in *Making Moral Decisions* in this series). They are the way in which *dharma* orders the nature-given human body, which itself becomes an expression of *dharma* and a way of patterning or ordering human behaviour. In rites of passage the body becomes a vehicle for the expression of tradition. The body, subject to genetic controls and the process of ageing, is constrained in ways determined by the tradition by means of the *saṃskāra*s, constraints which are, in fact, perceived to facilitate a person's growth or development through time. The general point about tradition's control of the body has been emphasised by D.M. Levin:

> Religion is a tradition of rituals which bind and fasten the body: it binds us to the performance of special tasks, special postures, gestures and movements; it dedicates the body to the incarnation of a spiritual life, promising that the body's careful adherence to such strict regulations will not be experienced, in the end, as its restriction, but rather, on the contrary, as its dream of health, well-being and liberation.[7]

While not liberating in the specific Hindu technical sense, the general idea of Levin's statement pertains to the *saṃskāra*s. While the body is certainly in many cases undergoing various inevitable, biological changes – at birth, puberty and death – these are defined and delineated by tradition through the *saṃskāra*s which use the body, and through the body, determine a person's 'state'. There are of course gender issues here, in that male and female bodies are constrained by *saṃskāra*s in different ways or by different, gender-specific rites. The *Dharma śāstra*s deal only with male rites of passage, but throughout India, women have undergone rites of passage based on oral or folk (*laukika*) traditions as V.K. Duvvury has shown with regard to South Indian Brahman women (Duvvury 1991: 102).

## The *saṃskāras*

For the high caste or 'twice-born' Hindu male, the theoretical model maintains that there are four stages of life through which he can pass: the student stage (*brahmacārya*), the householder stage (*gṛhastha*), the forest-dweller stage (*vānaprastha*) and the renouncer stage (*saṃnyāsa*). The first two stages are concerned with worldly life, the third with a life retired from household duties, and the last with world transcendence and salvation. This scheme is, however, a theoretical model and most Hindus do not, and perhaps have never, passed through it in an ordered sequence; most remain as householders, while some become renouncers without ever having been householders.

Each of these states or *āśrama*s is a 'state': a stable social condition which lasts for a significant period of time within a person's life, which defines the kind of person one is, and defines the social and religious possibilities which are open to one. The term 'state' is wider, however, than the Sanskrit *āśrama*, in that it incorporates all stages of human development, whereas *āśrama* refers only to states of being after initiation in childhood. Moreover the last *āśrama* is not technically accessed by a rite of passage, for the *saṃskāra*s are concerned purely with social life and not with liberation.

The junctures between states from birth, or before, until after death, are marked by rites of passage. At each of these junctures, the Hindu undergoes a ritual process of purification and is made ready for the next stage in his life. As R. Pandey says, the *saṃskāra*s are 'for sanctifying the body, mind and intellect of an individual, so that he may become a full-fledged member of the community' (Pandey 1969: 16). They are the processes between states, marking off the major transition points in a person's biography at birth, during youth (perhaps at puberty but not necessarily so), marriage and death. The *saṃskāra*s also mark out less significant transition points within childhood, which do not indicate any radical, ontological shifts. For example, the ritual of the child's first outing is lower in significance than the rite of becoming a member of high caste society.

The system of *saṃskāra*s is a 'liturgical order' in Rappaport's sense of the term,[8] in that it is an invariant sequence making up a complete cycle and controlling the unfolding householder's biography. The performance of a *saṃskāra* entails the implicit acceptance of the other rites, of *dharma* and of the Hindu orthoprax value system. The actual number of *saṃskāra*s varies in different *Dharma śāstra*s, but the important point is that, although there are specific variations, the totality of the *saṃskāra*s is a ritual sequence or complete system which expresses *dharma*. Up to forty are recorded in the *Gautama-dharma-śāstra*, though the standard number in the *Gṛhya Sūtra*s is from between twelve and eighteen (Pandey 1969: 17–24). The *Manusmṛti* (2.16; 26; 29; 3.1–4) mentions thirteen, though sixteen is the standard number, a number which itself has magical connotations.[9] Access to these *saṃskāra*s is dependent upon class and gender, and only brahman males can perform all of them.

The significance of Hindu rites of passage is that their performance entails a brahmanical value system and acceptance of brahmanical distinctions between those who can perform the rites and those who cannot. The *saṃskāra*s underline, implicitly if not explicitly, differences in gender roles and social classes or castes. Indeed, it has been argued that the primary function of rites of passage is not so much to ensure the temporal transition between states, for example from childhood to adulthood, but to ensure the separation of social groups; to ensure the separation between 'those who have undergone it, not from those who have not yet undergone it, but from those who will not undergo it in any sense, and thereby instituting a lasting difference between those to whom the rite pertains and those to whom it does not pertain'.[10] The high caste boy who undergoes the vedic initiation or *upanayana* ceremony is separated not only from his younger contemporaries who have not yet undergone the rite, but also, and for life, from those castes and from women, who are not eligible to undergo the rite.

The standard list of sixteen *saṃskāra*s implies these distinctions and exclusions. We shall here list the standard sixteen *saṃskāra*s, before going on to discuss some in more detail and more general issues.

The first three are prenatal rites, followed by birth, childhood and educational rites, then marriage and lastly death rites. 1. *Garbhādhāna*, the rite of the 'conception of the embryo', or the 'infusion of semen' performed at the time of conception. 2. *Puṃsavana*, the rite of 'bringing forth a boy', performed with a pregnant woman to ensure the birth of a male child. 3. *Sīmantonnayana*, the rite of 'parting the hair' of the pregnant woman during the fourth, sixth or eighth month of her pregnancy in order to ensure her well-being and to protect her from inauspicious spirits. 4. *Jātakarman*, the birth rite for the safe delivery of the child. 5. *Nāmakaraṇa*, the name-giving rite on the tenth or twelfth day after birth. 6. *Niṣkramana*, the child's first outing on an auspicious day. 7. *Annaprāśana*, the rite of first feeding the child solid food. 8. *Chūḍākaraṇa*, the rite of tonsure during the first or third year. 9. *Karṇavedha*, the ear-piercing ceremony between three and five. 10. *Vidyārambha*, the learning of the alphabet when the child is between five and seven. 11. *Upanayana*, the rite of initiation and investiture of the sacred thread from about eight up to about twenty-four. 12. *Vedārambha*, the rite of beginning vedic study. 13. *Keśānta*, the first shaving of the beard. 14. *Samāvartana*, the formal end to student life. 15. *Vivāha*, the marriage rite. And finally, 16. *Antyeṣṭi*, the funeral rites.

Of these the most important transition points for the high caste Hindu, apart from birth, have been the initiation ceremony (*upanayana*), which marks out the transition from childhood to high caste society, the marriage ceremony (*vivāha*), marking out the beginning of the householder's life, and the funeral rites (*antyeṣṭi*), which mark the end of the householder's life and the beginning of a new existence. In contemporary Hinduism, very often the *upanayana* and marriage ceremonies are conflated for reasons of economy, particularly in urban areas. We shall here examine four of these processes: the birth, youth, marriage and funeral *saṃskāra*s.

## THE BIRTH RITES

In contrast to death, which is inauspicious (*aśubha*), birth for a Hindu is a joyous and auspicious (*śubha*) occasion. The bringing forth of a child, especially a boy, is a sacred duty incumbent upon all married couples, yet, like death, it is associated with danger and impurity (*aśuddhi*). All products of the body, such as hair, nails, blood and semen, are impure for the Hindu, and the process of birth is therefore polluting (Madan 1987: 56). As Louis Dumont notes, 'impurity corresponds with the organic aspect of man' (Dumont 1980: 50) and those who service impurity, the washer castes who wash the soiled linen after a birth, live in a constant state of impurity which the high caste householder enters only briefly. The biological process of birth needs to be contained and controlled within a ritual structure in order to limit and even negate the effects of pollution. Indeed, Manu says that the performance of the birth rite of passage counteracts the birth pollution caused through conception (the mixing of semen and blood) (Manu 2.27).

Hindu rites of passage can be seen to follow the pattern of separation from the previous state, margin or transition, and aggregation or reintegration into the new state. With a first pregnancy a woman generally leaves the marriage home and goes to the home of her parents after the *sīmantonnayana*, the rite of parting the hair, thereby physically separating herself from her previous condition. Although preparation preceded the birth by a month or so, the actual performance of the birth ceremony (*jātakarman*) was begun, according to Manu, before the severing of the umbilical cord

(Manu 1.29). The actual ceremony comprises a number of rites to ensure the production of intelligence or wisdom in the child, long life and strength (Pandey 1969: 75–7). According to the *Āśvalāyana Gṛhya-sūtra*, the first is achieved by the father muttering in the child's ear, invocations to the deities Sāvitrī, Sarasvatī and the Āśvins; long-life by feeding the child honey and clarified butter on a golden spoon; and strength by touching the baby's shoulders and reciting a vedic verse (*Āśvalāyana Gṛhya-sūtra* 1.15.1–3). After the baby's birth a woman might remain at her parent's home for some months, before being reincorporated into her marriage home again with the new, higher status of mother, especially higher if she is the mother of a male child.

Because of the pollution of birth, which lasts for a period of about ten days, both mother and child are in danger from evil spirits (*grāha*) and ceremonies are performed to protect them. To mark the end of this period of impurity – the liminal period when the mother is truly outside of 'ordinary' human transactions – a Brahman priest might sprinkle the house with a sprig of mango from a pot containing holy water (Duvvury 1991: 184ff.) This is followed by the naming ceremony (*nāmakaraṇa*) on about the eleventh day.

Undoubtedly, throughout Indian history and in contemporary India the birth of a boy, particularly a first child, is regarded as more auspicious than the birth of a girl, though this is not to say that the birth of a girl is regarded as inauspicious. When a man sees his son he has repaid his debt to the ancestors (Manu 9.106). Duvvury gives a good example of the importance of a son among the Aiyars, the Tamil-speaking orthodox or Smārta Brahmans, among whom it is believed that with the birth of a son, the first of three generations of ancestors pass over from the intermediate realm of the ancestors (*pitṛloka*) into the world of heaven (*svargaloka*). She writes that upon the birth of a son the father 'feels relieved that he has at last done his duty to the manes of his forefathers and has enabled his line to attain immortality' (Duvvury 1991: 182). Indeed, the *Āśvalāyana Gṛhya-sūtra* (1.6.1) even says that the birth of a son brings purification to twelve descendants as well as twelve ancestors on both the husband's and wife's sides. Such a son will grow and pass through the various childhood rites of naming, first outing, tonsure and so on, until he reaches the time for initiation into caste society, a very important rite of passage.

## THE HIGH CASTE INITIATION (*UPANAYANA*)

This is of great significance for the high caste male in that it marks his entry into caste society and makes him a *dvija*, 'twice-born'. According to the ritual literature, the *upanayana* rite was performed between the ages of eight and twenty-four, depending upon class. The *Āśvalāyana Gṛhya-sūtra* states that a Brahman boy should be between eight and sixteen, a *kṣatriya* between eleven and twenty-two and a *vaiśya* between twelve and twenty-four (1.19.1–7; cf. Manu 2.36). The text even says that it is not possible to initiate youths beyond these ages and such a person would be cut off from the community, having lost his right to learn the vedic *mantra*s (1.19.8). In contemporary India, attitudes are less strict, and many take initiation just before their marriage when they may be older than the textually prescribed age limits. Indeed, holding the *upanayana* on the day before the wedding is common practice. It is therefore not appropriate to call the *upanayana* ritual a 'puberty' rite, as it may occur well before puberty or long after, though its significance of formal entry into the community may well be akin to puberty rites in other cultures. The ceremony might also accompany the marriage of a female relative, partly on economic grounds to avoid too many long journeys for relatives who live at a distance. This is especially important in Britain, where relatives might travel from India for an *upanayana* or wedding.

That the *upanayana* rite separates the boy from childhood and brings him into closer proximity to adulthood is also significant in that it excludes him from other spheres of social life and activity. Through undergoing the *upanayana*, the high caste boy is being separated from the world of women, who are excluded from undergoing the rite, and the sphere of the mother, legitimising gender distinctions and roles. Indeed, this rite implies a Hindu cosmological symbolism which legitimises social structure and gender roles: male is to female as sun is to moon, Śiva to Śakti, and spirit (*puruṣa*) to matter (*prakṛti*), a hierarchical symbolism in which the former term is always higher than the latter.[11]

Through the high caste boy's distinction being highlighted, there is a large group of people, the non-twice-born castes, whose exclusion is thereby underlined. The rite excludes a vast body of low caste Hindus from the higher echelons of Hindu culture. In performing the *upanayana*, the high caste boy is acceding to the brahmanical value system which entails the exclusion of the impure castes. Again, the rite taps into a cosmological symbolism in which the lower class emerge from the feet of the giant male person at the beginning of the world, while the higher classes emerge from his thighs, shoulders and mouth (see 'Hinduism' in *Making Moral Decisions* in this series). But to return to the rite itself.

The *upanayana* ceremony usually takes a whole day, during which time the initiate sits with the officiating priest before the sacred fire, before a sacred tree, and before a large pot, symbol of the Goddess. Although ritual details vary in classical texts as well as regionally, the general pattern is that the boy's head is shaved except for the tuft on the crown, he is then bathed and given a *kaupīna* or loin cloth, and the boy's father brings him into the presence of the priest and the fire pit or metal container in which the sacred fire is kindled. Oblations are offered to the fire and a girdle or cord is tied around the boy's waist. For a Brahman this was traditionally made of *muñja* grass, for a *kṣatriya*, a bow-string, and for a *vaiśya*, it was made of wool. He also traditionally wears an antelope skin over his shoulders or clothing of various colours depending on caste, and holds a sacred staff, the symbol of the vedic student. These rites are accompanied by the recitation of vedic *mantra*s by the officiating Brahman.

The boy takes a vow of celibacy, and then follows the most important part of the *upanayana*: the investiture of the sacred thread, the symbol of twice-born (*dvija*) status, worn over the right shoulder and renewed each year during the month of *śravan* (August), until either death or renunciation (*saṃnyāsa*). After the investiture of the thread, which comprises a number of strands, usually three or five, joined by a single knot, the boy is taught the famous 'root *mantra*' (*mūlamantra*), the Gāyatrī, which thenceforth is recited daily at dawn by Brahmans,[12] and he receives a secret name. He will also learn the procedures for making offerings into the sacred fire (*homa*). At the end of the ceremony, the 'departure' for Kāśī (i.e., Varanasi) is the symbolic gesture of leaving for the religious centre of Hinduism in order to study. The boy, however, is 'persuaded', sometimes with some mirth, by his maternal uncles not to go, but rather to remain and be tempted by the promise of a bride. This is then followed by a feast in contemporary Hindu households, and the giving of gifts to the boy.

An elaborate and rich symbolism is entailed in these rites, each ritual object having layers of symbolic resonance. The strands of the sacred thread, for example, are said to represent the three qualities (*guṇa*) of nature (*prakṛti*), namely lightness (*sattva*), darkness (*tamas*) and passion (*rajas*), or the three debts owed by a Hindu to the ancestors, the gods and the seers (see 'Hinduism' in *Making Moral Decisions* in this series). An elaborate colour symbolism is involved in these rites. For example, the colour of the upper garment worn by the boy traditionally reflected different classes. The law books state that reddish clothing should be worn by a Brahman, a different shade of red (dyed with madder) should be worn by a *kṣatriya* and yellow should be worn by a *vaiśya* (*Āpasthamba Gṛhya-sūtra* 1.19.10).

Traditionally, the *upanayana* marked the entry into the celibate, student stage of life (*brahmacārya*) and, according to Pandey, originally meant no more than going to a teacher and asking to be admitted as his student (Pandey 1969: 114), though its later significance is undoubtedly that the young man becomes a high caste member. As a student, he repays his innate debt of vedic study to the seers (*ṛṣi*) and a further rite is performed, usually the day following his initiation, of 'beginning vedic study' (*vedārambha*). According to the traditional model, the end of vedic study is marked by the *samāvartana saṃskāra*, during which the *guru* is paid a fee (*dakṣinā*). The young man takes a bath, thereby becoming a *snātaka*, 'one who has bathed', and becomes eligible for marriage (Manu 2.245–6; 3.4). He is not practically a complete member of his caste until his marriage, though after his initiation he is empowered to learn and hear the Veda, and, once married, to perform the vedic daily and occasional rituals. Indeed, there are solemn obligations attached to the wearing of the sacred thread invested during this time, namely, the obligation to perform one's ritual duty (*dharma*) according to one's caste and stage of life, and the obligation to avoid pollution. The high caste Hindu will adhere strictly to caste rules of endogamy and commensality.

The *upanayana* gives a high caste boy access to resources within the tradition, which allows him to develop into a full member of his society and to experience its richness. After initiation he can, and indeed must, learn the Veda, the sacred revelation, and perform its ritual injunctions such as, after marriage, maintaining the sacred household fires which he must do for the rest of his householder's life. Manu (2.170–71) says that 'the sun-god is spoken of as his mother and the teacher as his father. The teacher is spoken of as the father due to his giving of the Veda, ritual action (*karman*) is not performed without the investiture of the sacred thread'.

While the *upanayana* is strictly for high caste boys according to the *śāstra*s, women were and are not excluded from membership of high caste communities. According to Manu, marriage is a woman's *upanayana*, and serving her husband is the equivalent of living with the vedic teacher, while housework is the woman's equivalent of the man's obligatory fire rituals (Manu 2.67)! But there are rites of passage for girls in Hindu communities at puberty, though these are not based on the Sanskrit textual tradition of the *śāstra*s, but on oral or folk traditions (*laukika*). It is important, as Julia Leslie has pointed out, not to see women in a South Asian context 'merely as the passive victims of an oppressive ideology but also (perhaps primarily) as the active agents of their own positive constructs'.[13]

In a recent study Duvvury has shown how Aiyar women have their own rites of passage, including an apparent equivalent of the *upanayana*. During their first menstruation, girls undergo an initiation (*tirandukuli*) which separates them from childhood. The initiation involves the girl being separated and isolated in a darkened room for three days (though with her friends for company, in the case cited by Duvvury 1991: 117), and lewd songs being sung by the older women of the community who have high status (*sumaṅgali*). On the fourth day the girl takes a ceremonial bath and a feast is held. She is also taken by her mother to the temple and to visit other households where the older women perform ceremonies (*arati*) for the young girl (Duvvury 1991: 120–32). The Aiyar girl is then in a 'liminal period' between childhood and motherhood, when she achieves a higher status and becomes 'auspicious' (*sumaṅgali*).

Such women's rites have probably long been a part of the Indian religious scene, but have largely gone unrecorded because of their 'folk' or *laukika* origins. Through these distinct rites of passage, women, says Duvvury, have been able to express their concerns and ambitions, though these are always within the context of a male-dominant social world. Women's concerns have almost always been on the leash of brahmanical orthopraxy. It must be remembered that in the dominant brahmanical ideology, the folk tradition is of lesser significance than the sacred Sanskrit, textual tradition. We have here a number of hierarchical distinctions implied between male/female, Sanskrit tradition (*śāstra*)/folk tradition (*laukika*), Sanskrit language/

vernacular languages, and universal law/human convention. Indeed, Duvvury claims that in expressing their concerns and hopes, women are ironically 'reinforcing man-made ideals of women in society', a society which 'continues to define women largely in terms of their functions as mothers and wives' (Duvvury 1991: 229).

## MARRIAGE

Unless a person becomes a renunciate, which may mean joining a monastic order, marriage (*vivāha*) has been the expected norm in Hindu communities. With the marriage *saṃskāra* the high caste young man enters fully into the householder's life and he can here pursue the human purposes (*puruṣārtha*) of duty (*dharma*), gaining wealth and worldly success (*artha*), and pursuing pleasure, particularly sexual pleasure (*kāma*). For a young Hindu woman marriage marks an end of her life with her parents and her childhood friends, and the beginning of a completely new life with her husband and his family, taking up the duties and expectations of a married woman and, ideally, giving birth to a son, perhaps the primary purpose of a Hindu marriage. Often a marriage ceremony, because of this rift with the past, is emotionally traumatic for a young girl who, indeed, is culturally expected to display some signs of sorrow at leaving her old way of life. Most Hindu girls will desire marriage, as a necessary transition into complete womanhood, but are nevertheless sad to leave their old life and home. Concerning the importance of marriage for the Hindu woman, Duvvury writes:

> For a woman, marriage is a journey to a new locality, status, role, group affiliation and set of relationships, and, above all, it is the only means to motherhood and integration into the world of women as well as into society as a whole. It is also an essential rite through which a woman can reach heaven.
>
> (Duvvury 1991: 138)

Marriage in Hinduism has a supreme social and religious significance. It theoretically unites families and provides the context in which to rear children, adhering to the religious and social norms appropriate to the particular caste. It also symbolises basic Hindu concepts such as the union of Śiva and Śakti, the male and female poles of the cosmos (Duvvury 1991: 139), and expresses at an interpersonal level the Hindu's transpersonal reality.

Marriage has been, and continues to be in the majority of Hindu homes, an arrangement between two families. The overriding concern, expressed in the law books, is not the emotional state of the young couple – whether or not they love each other – but their social status, educational and economic compatibility. Indeed, I have heard it said that a Hindu youth does not marry the girl he loves, but loves the girl he marries. Marriage based on choice due to an affective bond, 'love-marriages' as they are called in India, is still the exception to the rule, even in cities in which there is much western influence. Such 'love-marriages' are regarded with a certain amount of humour and curiosity, though they are not without precedent in Indian society. There may have been a tradition of noble girls choosing their own husbands in a ritual gathering (*svayamvara*), the most famous instance of which is Damayantī's choice of Nala in the Nala episode in the *Mahābhārata* (see 'Hinduism' in *Making Moral Decisions* in this series). Manu, too, in his list of eight kinds of marriage lists the *gandharva* marriage, in which a couple have sex due to mutual desire (Manu 3.32).[14]

Compatibility in terms of caste is the most important factor to be considered in a marriage, though other factors are taken into account, such as wealth, occupation and the respective horoscopes of the boy and girl. Manu specifies that families should check the health of the potential bride's family, ensuring that there is no disease, that they do not have hairy bodies (!), and have not abandoned the vedic rites (Manu 3.7). Marriage is not taken lightly in Hindu communities, and the families involved are generally eager to ensure a good match, which primarily means the families' social compatibility.

Within caste (*jāti*), marriage is mostly endogamous, yet generally exogamous with regard to kin-group (*gotra*), usually within one village. That is, in rural India, while marrying within a caste, a person will marry outside of their village. Manu says that a twice-born man should marry a girl of the same class (*varṇa*) who has the appropriate characteristics (*lakṣana*), by which he means is a virgin and, while being within the caste, is outside of the kin-group or family lineage (*gotra*) (Manu 3.4–5).

The social realities of marriage among Hindus are, however, more complex than Manu's prescriptions, and there are many regional differences within India of the relation between marriage and kinship. For example, cross-cousin marriage is desirable in the South among the people who speak Dravidian languages, but is undesirable in the north among the speakers of Indo-Aryan languages (see Dumont 1980: 111). Another notable exception to caste endogamy is among the Nambuthiri Brahmans of Kerala. Here the oldest son in a family marries a Nambuthiri woman, but the remaining sons maintain alliances with the low caste Nayar women. The children from these alliances belong to the Nayar caste, living in the house of their mother and mother's brother. Their Brahman father might visit the house, though he would, of course, bring his own food and utensils, for to eat with non-Brahmans, even his 'family', would be polluting (Dumont 1980: 119).

The marriage *saṃskāra* is the most important rite in a Hindu's life and is an elaborate occasion. The marriage of a daughter, involving as it does the giving of gifts to the bridegroom's family, is an occasion involving great expense and, according to Dumont, is the main cause of debt in rural India, 'so imperative are the dictates of prestige, even for the poor' (Dumont 1980: 110). A marriage ceremony is an opportunity to display a family's wealth, and expresses the hierarchical relations between groups, not only between castes, but also between families. In this social hierarchy usually the bride's family have a lower status than the bridegroom's who, almost expectedly, will criticise the proceedings organised by the bride's father.

The actual process of the marriage *saṃskāra* will vary in different regions to some extent, for marriage ceremonies are a mixture of both vedic and folk elements, though the essentials, such as the couple circumambulating the sacred fire, remain constant. The marriage ceremony itself is quite simple, though the entire wedding may take several days of festivities. The rite takes place in a booth constructed traditionally of banana and mango leaves and begins with the formal giving away of the bride by her father to the groom and his father. As Duvvury says, in Hindu perception, 'one of the greatest gifts a man can bestow on another is the gift of a virgin daughter in marriage', for which he will obtain good *karman* or merit (*puṇya*) (Duvvury 1991: 137). Singing songs of blessing follows this ceremony, which in turn is followed by oblations being offered to the sacred fire before which the couple sit. The bride's wrist is tied with a thread and she places her foot three times on the groom's family grinding stone, a gesture which represents fidelity. The couple then take seven steps (*saptapadi*) around the fire, the bride following the groom. The *homa* or making offerings to the sacred fire, which the groom learned at his *upanayana*, is then performed by the groom with his bride. If the ceremony is in the evening, the couple might go out to see the pole star, Dhruva, and the bride will vow to be constant like the pole star. The wedding feast then continues.

Eventually when the proceedings are over, the bride will return to her husband's home to take on her new role in the extended family as wife, daughter-in-law and, probably within a short time, as mother. The birth of a son will give the couple, particularly the woman, high status and they will have truly embarked on the state of the householder, the *gṛhasthāśrama*.

## FUNERAL RITES

If a householder does not become a renouncer, then when he dies his body will undergo a funeral. Death, as in most cultures, is inauspicious in Hinduism and a death in the family, as L.A. Babb observes, brings the twofold danger of pollution and a potentially malevolent ghost (Babb 1975: 90). The last *saṃskāra* attempts to neutralise this pollution and danger by reintegrating the family back into the social context from which they have been momentarily separated, and allowing the spirit of the dead to travel on its way, leaving the family in peace.

While the concerns of bereavement, the neutralising of death-pollution and the freeing of the spirit from worldly attachments are pan-Hindu concerns, the actual funerary rites vary to some extent in different regions of India and in different castes. Cremation is usual, though among lower castes inhumation takes place and children and holy men are generally not cremated but buried. Indeed, a holy man, having previously undergone his own symbolic funeral at renunciation, might be simply immersed in a river, having transcended his social identity.

A dying person, having received the gift of holy water (preferably from the Ganges), is taken outside the house to die under the open sky. A general pattern of funerary rites is for the corpse to be washed and cremated on the same day as the death. The corpse is bathed, anointed with sandal-wood paste, traditionally shaved if male, dressed or wrapped in a cloth, and carried to the cremation ground by male friends and relatives who, in contrast to western funeral processions, move as quickly as possible, chanting the name of God (e.g., 'Rām'). On the funeral pyre, often by a river in which the ashes may later be immersed, the corpse's feet are directed to the realm of Yama, the god of death, to the south, and the head to the realm of Kubera, Lord of riches, in the north. A pot may be broken by the body's head, symbolising the release of the soul. According to the law books, from three to five fires, which were the householder's sacred fires, kindle the bier, and the destiny of the deceased can be predicted from which of the fires reaches the body first (*Āśvalāyana Gṛhya-sūtra* 4.4.1–5). The remains of the body are gathered up between three to ten days after the funeral and either buried or immersed in a river, preferably the holy Ganges (Babb 1975: 93ff; Pandey 1969: 234–63).

In the days immediately following a death, the family are polluted. This pollution lasts for a varying period of time during which *śraddha* ceremonies are performed. These are offerings of rice balls to the deceased in order to construct and feed its body in the afterlife. This body is complete ten days later and the family are released from the most dangerous death-pollution. Between thirteen days and a year after death, the final offering of rice balls (*piṇḍa*) is made at the *sapiṇḍikaraṇa* rite. Significantly, ten days elapse between death and the final formation of the *preta* body, which, Knipe observes, recapitulates the ten lunar months of the embryo's gestation.[15] The final *sapiṇḍikaraṇa* rite at the end of the life-cycle rituals can therefore be seen to be homologous with the birth rite at the beginning of life. Once the *sapiṇḍikaraṇa* is completed the deceased is released from the intermediate world of the 'ghosts' (*pretaloka*) to the realm of the ancestors (*pitṛloka*).[16] The cycle of rites of passage is thus completed.

## Sanskritisation and the *saṃskāra*s

The *saṃskāra*s have performed, and continue to perform, a number of functions within Hindu society. They not only mark off critical transition points in a human biography, which may correspond to times of biological and psychological crisis and change (at birth, puberty and death for example), but they also reflect Hindu systems of symbolic classification and so are about establishing Hindu value systems and a system of social acceptance and exclusion. Through the *saṃskāra*s a person becomes familiar with the social status of different actors, his or her own place in the community, and the regulation of gender roles.

Although there are regional variations, the *saṃskāra*s reflect the extraordinary success of the dominant brahmanical ideology, which permeates nearly all levels of social life. This process whereby the brahmanical ideology of *dharma* becomes the central guiding force in many people's lives is known as Sanskritisation; the process whereby rituals, deities and ideas contained in orthodox Sanskrit treatises become assimilated by local, folk traditions. The *saṃskāra*s are derived from this literature and reflect brahmanical values which are implicitly accepted by the Hindu through participating in these rites, particularly in so far as they distinguish between purity and impurity. For example, the birth *saṃskāra*, through highlighting the distinction between purity and impurity, conveys a message about hierarchical gender relations and status. The ideal child is male and the father performs rites upon his wife; that is, although she gives birth, she has a minimal ritual function. The *saṃskāra*s also establish brahmanical values through the exclusion of lower castes (the non-twice-born), who are too impure to perform them, except for the marriage *saṃskāra*, which is open to all. Through marriage, the entrance to the householder's life, even the lower castes are brought within the sphere of brahmanical influence and implicit acceptance of its value system. Indeed, to perform one *saṃskāra* is to adhere implicitly to the total ritual cycle, even though one might be excluded from particular rites because of caste or gender.

The Hindu rites of passage therefore contain implicit ideas about the nature of human life, social structure and destiny as represented in the ideal of *dharma*, with its two focuses of performing one's correct caste duty and adhering to behaviour appropriate to one's stage of life (see 'Hinduism' in *Making Moral Decisions* in this series). They underline social difference and emphasise the distinction of some groups from others; of the dominant groups from the subordinate ones.

With the funeral *saṃskāra* the cycle of Hindu rites of passage is at an end. Although the system of *saṃskāra*s is total and complete in itself, there are nevertheless other occasional rituals which a Hindu might perform. These are the ritual of renunciation (*saṃnyāsa*), the last stage of life, and optional sectarian initiations (*dīkṣā*) as a householder or renouncer.

As we have seen, there is a distinction within Hinduism between, on the one hand, liberation and, on the other, the householder's life in the world. The *saṃskāra*s are concerned exclusively with the latter. They are not conducive to liberation and are of social and dharmic significance only. By contrast, renunciation and sectarian initiation are generally for the purpose of eventual liberation.

## Sectarian initiation

Rites of passage are not concerned with liberation. As we noted at the beginning of this chapter, the worlds of salvation and social transaction are clearly distinct. As a householder, the Hindu is concerned mainly with the maintenance of caste boundaries, the maintaining of the sacred fires and the performance of the *saṃskāra*s. Unlike the renouncer, he is not generally concerned with the path to salvation. However, should the householder aspire towards liberation, there are sectarian initiations which claim to lead to that goal. Sectarian initiations are open both to the householder and to the renouncer. Such initiations are not part of the normative Hindu rites of passage, but can function in a similar way, giving a person access to traditions and teachings which were previously closed to him. An example can be given from Śaivism.

In Śaiva Siddhānta, a Hindu tradition flourishing particularly in South India, centred on the worship of the deity Śiva in his form as Sadāśiva, there are essentially two initiations: into the tradition and into liberation. The initiation into the tradition, the *samaya-dīkṣā*, gives access to the cult of Śiva, bestowing on the initiate, who becomes a 'son of Śiva', or *putraka*, the right to hear certain texts, and requiring him to perform certain daily, obligatory rituals. This initiation might at some time be followed by the *nirvāṇa-dīkṣā* which gives access to liberation. After this rite the initiate will perform obligatory daily rituals until death when he will be liberated by the grace of Śiva.

## Renunciation

Not technically a rite of passage, renunciation, the last of the Hindu stages of life (*āśrama*), is such an important institution within Hinduism that it needs to be mentioned here. The ritual of renunciation is undoubtedly a 'process' between two distinct 'states', which marks the boundary between the condition of caste member with legal and moral obligations, and the condition of castelessness, traditionally beyond legal obligations. The renouncer is in some ways therefore akin to the non-twice-born Hindu, for renunciation entails going beyond caste and renouncing social obligation in order to achieve, eventually, salvation or freedom (*mokṣa*). The householder is clearly a social being, with defined duties and responsibilities, while the renouncer is not a social being in the same sense, having no obligations to family and caste, though he nevertheless depends upon the community for his livelihood, gives teachings and perhaps lives in a monastic community.

As has been noted by a number of scholars (e.g., Dumont 1980) there is a tension between the ideals of renunciation in which the ascetic feels disgust for the world and cultivates detachment, and those of the householder who cultivates the goals (*artha*) of duty, worldly success and pleasure (see 'Hinduism' in *Making Moral Decisions* in this series). Rites of passage in the sense of the *saṃskāra*s might therefore be seen as essentially life-affirming, while the rite and institution of renunciation as essentially life-denying. This can be seen in texts on renunciation which describe the ritual act, such as the *Treatise on World Renunciation*, which even advocates suicide by, among other means, starvation in order to be free from the suffering of the world.[17] This text describes how the renouncer should deposit the sacrificial fires, which he has kept all his life as a householder, within himself, discard or burn the sacrificial thread, shave his head and take up the minimal possessions of the renunciate.

What is of interest here is that the ritual of renunciation, the liminal phase between two socially defined states, is almost the reverse of the *upanayana* ceremony. The renouncer is, as it were, undoing the adult, caste identity imposed upon him through that rite as a boy or young man. The ritual of renunciation can be contrasted therefore with the *saṃskāra*s as a whole and the *upanayana* in particular. As the *upanayana* excludes certain groups of people and makes a statement about identity within a hierarchical social structure, so the rite of renunciation draws a clear line between those within the dharmic realm, and so within the realm of *saṃsāra*, and those who are, symbolically at least, beyond that world on their way to liberation. The Hindu rites of passage say as much about human nature and destiny by what is excluded from them as by what is included. Their primary concern is the world of human transaction, the relation between social groups and genders, and providing the expression of an ethical resource for Hindu householders. The realm of salvation is not their concern, though that realm, the realm of the world-renouncer, derives its meaning only due to those worldly concerns. The *saṃskāra*s are as important for what they say by excluding certain groups and ideas, as for what they include. Yet ultimately the *saṃskāra*s and what they represent, must, in the dominant Hindu ideology, be eventually left behind. In the householder/renouncer distinction, the renouncer is ultimately superior to the householder, because he is indifferent to the phenomenal universe and is fulfilling life's highest purpose, its transcendence. Yet the householder's world-affirmation through the system of the *saṃskāra*s, is the social foundation of this ideology which is its own negation: the 'inner conflict' of the tradition[18] which has produced such creative tension within Hinduism and throughout the history of South Asia.

NOTES

1. Bell, C. (1992) *Ritual Theory, Ritual Practice*, New York, Oxford University Press, pp. 69–71.
2. Piatigorsky, A. (1985) 'Some phenomenological observations on the study of Indian religions', in R. Burghardt and A. Cantille (eds) *Indian Religion*, London, Curzon Press, pp. 215–17.
3. See Gombrich, R. (1988) *Theravada Buddhism*, London & New York, Routledge and Kegan Paul, pp. 25–7.
4. Bourdieu, P. (1992) *Language and Symbolic Power*, Cambridge, Polity Press, chapter 4.
5. See Carman, J.B. and Marglin, F.A. (eds) (1985) *Purity and Auspiciousness in Indian Society*, Leiden, Brill.
6. Rappaport, R.A. (1992) 'Ritual, time and eternity', *Zygon*, 27, 1: 7.
7. Levin, D.M. (1985) *The Body's Recollection of Being*, London, Routledge, p. 180ff.

8. Rappaport, 'Ritual, time and eternity', p. 7.
9. See Gonda, J. (1985) 'The number sixteen', in *Change and Continuity in Indian Religion*, Delhi, Munshiram Manoharlal.
10. See Bourdieu, *Language and Symbolic Power*, p. 117.
11. See Bourdieu, *Language and Symbolic Power*, p. 118.
12. The Gāyatrī mantra, named after its meter, the *gāyatrī*, from the *Ṛg-veda* (3.62.10), is:

    *Om. bhūr, bhuva, sva,*
    *tat savitur varenyam*
    *bhargo devasya dhīmahi*
    *Dhiyo yo naḥ pracodayāt.*

    (Om, earth, atmosphere, sky. May we contemplate the desirable light of the god Savitṛ. May he inspire our thoughts.)

13. Leslie, J. (1991) *Roles and Rituals For Hindu Women*, London, Pinter Publishers, p. 1.
14. Manu gives accounts of eight kinds of marriage and the various punishments for marrying outside of class prescriptions, yet at the same time allows for some variation and human weakness. For example, the text says both that a Brahman can marry a *śūdra* and that a Brahman cannot marry a *śūdra* (3.13–16). The ideal is the high caste, arranged marriage, but there are some circumstances in which different kinds of 'marriage' are appropriate, while some kinds of marriage are always to be condemned. The eight kinds of marriage are named after Brahmā, the gods (*daiva*), the sages (*ṛṣayaḥ*), the Lord of Creatures, the demons (*asurāḥ*), the heavenly musicians (*gandharvāḥ*), ogres (*rākṣasāḥ*), and the ghouls (*paiśācāḥ*). Of these, the first six pertain to the Brahman, the last four to the ruler and the last three to the commoner (Manu 3.21–23). The first four describe different ways of the father giving away his daughter as a bride, the demonic law refers to a man who wants a girl out of desire and gives much wealth to her relatives, the *gandharva* marriage is simply a girl and her lover uniting out of desire for each other, and the ghoulish marriage is a man having sex with a girl who is asleep, drunk or mad (Manu 3.27–34).
15. Knipe, D. (1977) 'Sapiṇḍikaraṇa: The Hindu rite of entry into heaven', in E. Reynolds and F.E. Waugh, *Religious Encounters with Death*, University Park, Pennsylvania State University Press.
16. Bowker, J. (1991) *The Meanings of Death*, Cambridge, Cambridge University Press, pp. 149–51. The idea of the deceased going to the realm of the ancestors after death, at one level seems to contradict the idea of reincarnation. Although there seems to be no cognitive

dissonance experienced by Hindus in this matter (some say that a soul is reborn from the realm of the ancestors), it perhaps indicates the autonomy of the ancient ritual realm, in contrast to a comparatively more recent ideology of reincarnation. See Wendy O'Flaherty (ed.) (1980) *Karma and Rebirth in Classical Indian Traditions*, Berkeley, University of California Press, pp. xviii–xx; 3–37.

17. Olivelle, P. (1977) *Vāsudevāśrama Yatidharmaprakāśa: A Treatise on World Renunciation* (2 vols), Vienna, Publications of the De Nobili Research Library, pp. 96–8.
18. See Olivelle, P. (1992) *The Saṃnyāsa Upaniṣads*, Oxford, Oxford University Press, pp. 19–23; Heesterman, J.C. (1985) *The Inner Conflict of Tradition: Essays in Indian Ritual, Kingship and Tradition*, Chicago, Chicago University Press.

## FURTHER READING

Babb, L.A. (1975) *The Divine Hierarchy*, New York and Oxford, Columbia University Press.

Buhler, G. (1987) *The Sacred Laws of the Aryans*, Delhi, AVF Books.

Dumont, L. (1980) *Homo Hierarchicus*, Chicago, University of Chicago Press.

Duvvury, V.K. (1991) *Play, Symbolism and Ritual: A Study of Tamil Brahmin Women's Rites of Passage*, New York, Peter Lang.

Fuller, C. (1992) *The Camphor Flame: Popular Hinduism and Society in India*, Princeton, Princeton University Press.

Madan, T.N. (1987) *Non-Renunciation*, Delhi, Oxford University Press.

O'Flaherty, W. (1991) *The Laws of Manu*, Harmondsworth, Penguin.

Pandey, R. (1969) *Hindu Saṃskāras*, Delhi, MLBD.

Stevenson, S. (1920) *The Rites of the Twice Born*, London, Oxford University Press.

# 4. Islam

*Clinton Bennett*

## Introduction

Plutarch (*c.* 46–120 CE), the Greek historian, once said, 'You may see states without walls, without laws, without coins, without writing, but a people without a God, without worship, without religious practices and sacrifices, hath no man seen'. Plutarch may have qualified his statement had he encountered a non-theistic religion such as Buddhism, but anthropologists and explorers and psychologists alike would probably agree that every social group so far encountered, studied and analysed by them marks life's most significant events with some ceremony or ritual observance. Usually, the term 'rites of passage' refers to rites surrounding birth, reception into the adult community, marriage and death. How different groups use symbol and ritual on these significant occasions usually expresses their deepest convictions about the meaning of human existence. Islam is no exception. As an all-embracing philosophy of life, it attaches profound meaning to these critical life-cycle events. Before describing how Muslims observe 'rites of passage', I shall introduce Islam's theological world-view; without this framework, we will not be able to appreciate how Islam's theological assumptions impact on everything Muslims do, including their marking of birth, marriage and death.

## Islam's world-view: creation

Islam always begins from its premise that God is the source of all life and that he (the Muslim word for God, Allāh, is a masculine word) has entrusted the human race with particular, even awesome, responsibilities. Muslims use the word *amānah* to describe this trust. It derives from their understanding of an important passage in the Qur'ān, Islam's scripture, which says that God created Adam as his *khalīfah*, trustee or vice-regent (*sūrah* 2:30). Qur'ān 33:73 elaborates: God offered this trust, *amānah*, to the heavens and to the earth, and to the hills, but they shrank away from it. He then offered the trust to man, 'and man assumed it'. What is this trust? It is delegated divine sovereignty (*al-wilayāt al-ilahiyya*), or authority, over his own environment, control of his own actions, the freedom to steward the earth's fruits wisely and well, or to 'do harm. . .' and to 'shed blood' which the angels feared of humanity at their creation: 'And when thy Lord said unto the angels: Lo, I am about to place a viceroy upon the earth, they said: Wilt Thou place therein one who will do harm therein and will shed blood, while we, we hymn thy praise and sanctify Thee?' (*sūrah* 2:30).

Muslims believe that Adam's very nature, how he had been made by God, gave him the innate ability to live in complete harmony with God's will. The term used to describe this innate at-one-ness with God is *fiṭrah* (literally 'primordial nature'), although the very Arabic word for man, *iḥsān*, from a root meaning 'companionable, agreeable, genial', also suggests at-one-ness (see Ruthven 1991: 126). The term *dīn-al-fiṭrah* is used as a synonym for Islam; Islam is 'the natural religion' because living in harmony with God and with one's fellow creatures is natural. Such ideal harmony, or peace (the word *Islām* is itself related to the Arabic word for 'peace', *salām*) reflects the very nature, or essence, of God himself. The most important word used to describe this essential nature is *tawḥīd* (harmony, balance, unity, or at-one-ness). God is *tawḥīd*. This is the very quality that human life was itself intended to reflect: a balance between enjoying earthly pleasures of food, drink and permitted sexual relations and labour (reflecting God's role as creator and sustainer), between this-worldly pursuits and spiritual pursuits (*'ibādāt*, or worship). In the Qur'ān, Adam chose to disturb this balanced and peaceful existence by eating the fruit of the forbidden tree. This introduces an important aspect of Islamic teaching, the concept that God has declared certain actions, or foods, permitted (*ḥalāl*) and some forbidden (*ḥarām*).

After disobeying God, Adam was expelled from the Garden but he was also forgiven: 'And He relented towards him' (*sūrah* 2:37). This primordial disobedience of Adam, then, in Islamic theology did not result in a fundamental change in humanity's essential (*fiṭrah*) ability to enjoy harmony with God; every human individual is still born with this innate innocence, or conformity with truth. Like Adam, all people possess the freedom to live in harmony with God's will, or to rebel against him, through disobedience. God also appointed Adam as his first prophet, giving him the gift of the *shahādah*, the divine formula (in Arabic) *Lā ilāha illā Llāh* (There is no God but God).

## The Islamic ideal

Islam teaches that from Adam's time onward, God constantly sent prophets to remind people of his will. Each received and preached the same essential message, the life-restoring *shahādah*, 'There is no God but God' or, as Muslims explain, 'There is no reality but the Reality' (see Schuon 1976: 16). During each prophet's lifetime, a second statement was added, 'And Noah, or Moses, or Jesus . . . is his messenger'. Finally, when the time was right for humankind to receive the definitive blueprint for individual and corporate living, God sent his last prophet, Muhammad (570–632 CE). With Muhammad's mission, the ideal model for human living was established: God 'perfected' and 'approved' Islam as the straight path for all people (*sūrah* 5:5). Now, the *shahādah* testifies, 'There is no God but God and Muhammad is his messenger'. We can translate this into theological language as, 'There is no will but God's Will, perfectly expressed through the prophet Muhammad'. Muslims regard Muhammad as the Universal prophet, as the Perfect Man (*iḥsān-i-kāmil*) and, significantly for this introduction to rites of passage in Islam, as 'the Lord of Adam's children'. Muslims not only recite the *shahādah*, but allow its impact to penetrate their inner being so that their will becomes completely re-tuned to the divine will and they cannot but live in complete harmony with their creator. Satan is warned away. Acceptance of the *shahādah* is the only condition of salvation in Islam. Glassé says, 'The *shahāda* expunges the error of Adam – symbolised by the eating of the forbidden fruit – of seeing objects as in reality, in place of God' (Glassé 1991: 359). There is also a link between reciting, almost 'breathing' the *shahādah*, and the breath of life that Allāh 'breathed' into Adam at the beginning of the human story (see *sūrah* 15:29 and 32:9).

Consequently, Muslim societies have as their model the early *ummah* (the community of Islam) under the leadership of the divinely inspired prophet, governed according to God's law. Just as the life of Muhammad provides the ideal for the life of each individual Muslim, so the corporate life of the *ummah* provides the model for Muslim society. Muslim children, born without guilt, will be surrounded from babyhood by reminders of God's blueprint. They will grow up constantly hearing the *shahādah*, so that its meaning will permeate their whole lives. Prayer, which God has ordained must be offered at five daily intervals (so that whether one is working or playing, every activity will be punctuated with moments of concentration on God alone), should become second nature as soon as possible. Ideally, Muslim family life, modelled on that of the Holy Family of Muhammad, will nurture *taqwā'*, 'God consciousness': a 'total frame of reference'.

The Muslim ideal, of course, assumes that Muslims will live in Muslim societies where the law of the land is the Law of Islam. In practice, not all Muslims actually live in Muslim countries. Today, too, there is also much debate about the actual content of Islamic Law. However, it remains true that whether they live in small family groups or in larger communities, Muslims will always try to emulate the example of Muhammad (his *sunnah*) and to observe *ādāb-al-Islām* (the customs of Islam) as faithfully as they can. In Islam, the customs, rites or ceremonies that mark life-cycle events share one basic aim: to remind Muslims that they are always before God, that he knows everything concerning them, even their most secret thoughts. The very mystery of life itself, given by God when he wills it, taken away by him when he wills it, the mystery of giving birth, of marital happiness, all rest with his infinite wisdom.

## Birth rite: greeting in the name of God

In any family of any faith or of none, the birth of a baby is usually a time of celebration and joy. In Islam, life is God's precious gift and the birth of a baby calls for thanksgiving and gratitude: 'No female beareth or bringeth forth save with His knowledge' (*sūrah* 35:11). As we shall see, Muslim tradition affords opportunity for parents to share their joy with relatives and friends. Islam regards marriage and having children as natural (*fiṭrah*), even as a religious duty. Muhammad married and fathered children, so his example gives important guidance as to how Muslims should behave at these times. The first tradition, or rite, surrounding the birth of a child is a simple but vital one. As soon as possible, the *shahādah* should be recited first in the child's right, then in his or her left ear. This will usually take place wherever the child is born, in the hospital or at home. It may be recited by the child's father although sometimes an *imām* will be invited to do this. *Imām*s are those Muslims who have studied the Qur'ān and *sharī'āh* and who are often paid by the community to lead prayers in the mosque, especially the community prayer on Friday when a sermon must also be preached. Usually, the *shahādah* is recited in the right ear in the slightly more elaborate form of the *adhān*, or the call to prayer that Muslims hear five times every day. This is what the *muazzin* cries from the mosque's minaret. The *adhān* begins with the words known as the *takbīr*, 'God is Greater' (*Allāhu Akbar*), repeated three times, then continues with the *shahādah* itself:

> I bear witness that there is no God but God
> I bear witness that there is no God but God,
> I bear witness that Muhammad is the Apostle of God.
> I bear witness that Muhammad is the Apostle of God . . .

Next, the invitation to pray:

> Come to prayers, come to prayers,
> Come to salvation, come to salvation [or 'come to the good']
> God is Greater, God is Greater.
> I bear witness that there is no God but God.

When repeated in the left ear the *shahādah* is usually recited in the form of the *iqāmah*. These are the words used at the very beginning of prayer, when the worshippers are standing shoulder to shoulder, and are often spoken by the *imām*. They are identical to the *adhān* except for the addition of the words, 'Prayers are now ready'. Obviously, the new-born child is unable to respond by performing the ritual prayer, *ṣalah*, as adult Muslims can, but by hearing this call to prayer, with its reminder that God is Absolute, the child's *fiṭrah* harmony with God is re-enforced by the sacramental power inherent in the sacred formula. The first word heard by the child is the '*Allāhu*' of the *takbīr*; thus the name of God greets his or her arrival in the world. The child becomes as Adam was.

Recitation of the *adhān* expresses the hope that, surrounded in infancy and childhood by parental love and by constant reminders of God's sovereignty, by the many qur'ānic expressions that Muslims are encouraged to use in daily life, children will soon want to respond to the summons themselves by joining the community in prayer. The importance of this pillar, or support, of faith (*īmān*) cannot be overstated. In Muslim tradition, Muhammad received the instructions regulating prayer during his *mir'āj*, night journey, when he was transported into the divine presence itself. Symbolically, then, prayer transports the worshippers into that presence. Muslims say that when they pray (and all faithful Muslims will be praying at the same time) they pray less as individuals than as representatives of the whole human race: 'in the *ṣalah* it is not the individual who prays, rather it is man as such, a representative of the species or all mankind recognising his relationship to the Almighty. Or it is creation, with the voice of man as a universal patriarch, praying to the Creator' (Glassé 1991: 348). *Ṣalah*, with the total prostration of the self before God, reminds Muslims that before the Absolute, they are as *'abd*, slaves. *'Ibādāh*, the word for worship (indeed for any permitted, as opposed to prohibited, activity) is derived from *'abd*.

The call to prayer also invites God's *'abd* to 'come unto salvation', or 'unto the good' (*falāh*). This is a reminder that *ṣalah* alone, without a righteous, moral life that is obedient to God in all areas, is worthless. Kenneth Cragg comments that *falāh* doesn't mean 'some pietistic abstraction or the indulgence of a private sanctity. It is the true state of well-being, the prosperity, of the people of God, fulfilled in communal existence and realised in social life. 'Come unto the good life', 'Alert yourself in mind and will to the authentic well-being of Muslim humanity, achieved within the Islamic order'. Such is the *falāh* as the *muazzin* proclaims and defines it' (Cragg 1986: 127). 'Come unto the good', recites the child's father, or the local *imām*, into the ear of the new-born child, meaning 'grow up as God's *'abd* and contribute to the well-being of the *ummah*'. This simple ritual, then, greeting the new-born child with the *shahādah*, expresses profound belief about the meaning of life as well as the hope that the child will continue to walk God's path. Muslims believe that children who die in infancy will return immediately to Paradise, having had no opportunity to do wrong.

## *'Aqīqah* and naming

Seven days after birth, another ritual is performed. Known as *'aqīqah*, it provides an opportunity for the family to share their joy with relatives and friends. This was the practice of the Prophet and so guidance is found in the *sunnah*. Probably no particular significance attaches to the 'seven' days; a week allows the family time to issue invitations and to prepare the festivities, although it was on the seventh day of creation that Allāh returned to his 'Throne' (*sūrah* 11:7; *sūrah* 25:59; *sūrah* 57:4) so the number seven does have special significance for Muslims, as it does for Jews. On the seventh day, according to this custom, which is thought to have been an ancient Arab one, the baby's head is shaved and the hair weighed. Later, an equivalent weight in gold or silver is given to the poor. The shaving of the head says that the baby is at one and the same time an *'abd* before God and a pure, innocent child yet untarnished by rebellious thoughts or immoral behaviour. The Prophet would often place a sweet in the child's mouth, usually a date which he would first chew into a pulp. Known as *taḥnīk*, this can also be interpreted as expressing something of the natural, unsullied 'sweetness' of a new-born child. After this, it is usual to offer a prayer for the child, in Arabic, a *du'ā*, or supplicatory prayer; God should be thanked and praised, health and blessing should be invoked. Next, festivities follow at which, traditionally, two sheep for a boy, one for a girl, are ritually slaughtered (with the words, 'In the name of God, O God, This is done for Your sake only'), cooked and eaten. A goat, cow, camel or ox can be slaughtered instead of a sheep. The 'two for a boy one for a girl' reflects the difference between men and women in inheritance rights: men receive two shares, women one (in Islam, maintenance of offspring and of dependent relatives is exclusively the responsibility of men). Custom says that one portion is for family, one for friends, while the third should be given to the poor. Thus, at this seventh day ceremony to celebrate the child's birth, the parents are twice reminded of those who are less blessed than they are. This sharing of joy even with the poor says that all people are creatures of God and we are one human family. It also reminds the couple that their social obligations reach beyond family and friends. This calls to mind Islam's fourth pillar, *zakāt*, the 'poor tax' – we only ever possess what we have as stewards.

Finally, at the *'aqīqah*, it is customary to name the child. This should be a 'beautiful and meaningful name', says one 'useful reference work for every Muslim family' (Al-Kaysi 1986). Recommended are the names of prophets, names 'consisting of two parts, the first of which is *'abd* (slave) compounded with one of Allāh's names are considered beautiful' (Al-Kaysi 1986: 131). Names suggesting sorrow or war should be avoided. Naming in Islam is regarded as an important responsibility; children should not be burdened with names that may cause embarrassment in later life. At creation, Adam was taught the names of all things, which even the angels did not know (*sūrah* 2:31). Again, this signifies Adam's position and responsibility as God's *khalīfah*. Glassé comments: 'Adam's knowledge of the names showed that he was, in fact, the synthesis of creation and at the same time its centre' (Glassé 1991: 42).

## Circumcision (*khitān*)

Muslim boys should be circumcised. This ancient tradition dates back to the time of Abraham, who, in the biblical account, was told by God to circumcise himself and all male members of his family as a visible sign of the covenant between his people and God. In that account, Ishmael, his oldest son, was about thirteen when circumcised. Muhammad is believed to be a descendant of Abraham and, among the Arabs, there appears to have been an ancient tradition of circumcision in the thirteenth year. In the Qur'ān, Abraham plays an important role. It was he, with Ishmael, who re-built and re-dedicated to God the shrine known as the *Ka'bah*, which many Muslims believe was the site of the garden in the creation narrative. Abraham is claimed as a true Muslim, who refused to worship the many gods of his peers: 'Abraham was not a Jew, nor yet a Christian, but he was an upright man who had surrendered to God' (*sūrah* 3:67). The Qur'ān itself does not refer to circumcision but it does refer to the covenant of which circumcision was the sign, see for example *sūrah* 2:83, 'And we made a covenant with the children of Israel, saying: worship none save Allāh, and be good to parents and to kindred and to orphans and the needy, and speak kindly to mankind, and establish worship and pay the poor due' but, says the qur'ānic account, the Jews back-slid. This description of the covenant religion, of course, actually anticipates Islam's own essential qualities, especially as exemplified in the life of Muhammad.

Circumcision, then, suggests that Islam is the true inheritor of the covenant relationship with God, who is the God of Jews, Christians and Muslims, 'Our God and your God is One, and unto Him we have surrendered' (*sūrah* 29:46). Some Muslim stories, or legends, say that Muhammad and a number of other prophets were born already circumcised. Today, Muslim boys are usually circumcised soon after the *'aqīqah* (it is sometimes combined with that ceremony), although they may be circumcised at any time between then and their thirteenth birthday. In some parts of the Muslim world, circumcision is accompanied by festivities. In Turkey, for example, boys dress up in colourful costumes for their circumcision (at about age eight) which takes place in a special circumcision palace. Adult converts to Islam are not obliged to be circumcised. Traditionally, if they wished to be circumcised they should perform the operation themselves, since it was thought improper for an adult man's penis to be seen by another man. However, strict rules of hygiene are always observed. Islam regards cleanliness and purity as virtues: 'God loves those who turn to Him and those who care for cleanliness' (*sūrah* 2:222). Muslims will often say that many of Islam's food prohibitions, circumcision and other Muslim traditions can be justified as much on grounds of health and hygiene as on any theological rationale.

## Why Islam has no initiation ceremony

Since being Muslim is *fiṭrah*, a child born of Muslim parents, raised in a Muslim family, and taught the Qur'ān from an early age, ought quite naturally to grow and to mature in his or her understanding of what it means to be God's *'abd*. Islam therefore has no equivalent of an initiation rite, except for non-Muslims who convert (Muslims prefer to say 're-vert', because all babies are naturally '*muslim*') to Islam. They will undergo a simple ceremony, usually in a mosque, when, before witnesses, they will be invited to recite the *shahādah*. Otherwise, there is no real concept of 'opting into' Islam, although there is freedom to 'opt out'. This aspect of Islam is often misunderstood. Islam involves not only external observation of its five obligatory (*farḍ*) duties, the five pillars, but also inner conviction and faith (*īmān*), verbally expressed in the *shahādah* and in other credal statements. God's gift of free will means that people can, if they wish, rebel against him. This, for someone nurtured since birth in Islam, means that they can choose to become a non-Muslim. *Sūrah* 2:256 says, 'there is no compulsion in religion'. Where misunderstanding does occur is with reference to the severe penalty, death, that can apply to Muslims who are accused and found guilty of 'apostasy', which seems to imply the lack of freedom to cease to be a Muslim. However, this only applies where *sharīʻah* law is fully established. In this context, to cease to be a Muslim is to reject the rule of law, yet, writes Mashuq Ibn Ally, 'a quiet desertion of Islamic duties is not a sufficient reason for inflicting death on a person. Only when the individual's desertion of Islam is used as a political tool for instigating a state disorder, or revolting against the law of Islam, can the individual apostate then be put to death as a just punishment for his act of treason and betrayal of the Muslim community' (Ibn Ally 1990: 26). This, of course, must be preceded by a successful prosecution before a properly constituted *sharīʻah* court.

For Muslims born and raised as Muslims, while there is no 'coming of age' rite, there will be several significant occasions in their growth towards adult faith. These include their first observance of the fast (*ṣawm*), the fast between dawn and dusk during the month of *Ramaḍān*, the first time they attend *Jumuʻah* (Friday) prayers in the mosque, and, stage by stage, their mastery of qur'ānic recitation. There are no mandatory ages for observing these but puberty is usually the point at which *ṣawm* becomes obligatory.

## Marriage

We have already noted that marriage is considered normal and natural in Islam. This is derived from the fact that God created Adam and his wife from a single soul. The Qur'ān says: 'your Lord created you from a single soul and from it created its mate and from them hath spread abroad a multitude of men and women' (*sūrah* 4:1), and 'Allāh created you from dust, then from a little fluid, then he made you pairs' (*sūrah* 35:11). Qur'ān 36:35 says, 'Glory be to Him who created all the sexual pairs'. Marriage, then, is *fiṭrah*, a reuniting of the male and female principles. Islam believes, therefore, that sex within marriage is wholesome and good and as much *'ibādāh* (worship) as any other permitted activity. One writer calls *'ibādah* 'the greatest purpose of marriage . . . The concept of *'ibādah*' he explains, 'is very wide. Every good deed, every service to humanity, every useful productive effort, and every good word is part of a true Muslim's worship of his creator' (Doi 1984: 116). Muslims also regard the family as the basic building block of society, so it is not surprising that 'it gives maximum attention to the family affairs of the believers' (Doi 1984: 129). Marriage, according to the Qur'ān, should be a relationship of *tawḥīd*, or of making one, of harmony between spouses, or, as *sūrah* 30:21 says, of 'love and mercy'. This verse refers to marriage as a 'sign from Allāh'. Marriage is meant to give comfort and joy to husband and wife and to provide the ideal environment in which children can be born, and raised to become good, pious Muslims.

Because it regards healthy marital relationships as essential for correct child rearing, and stable family life as necessary for the proper functioning of society itself, Islam does not view marriage as merely a matter for private or personal choice. This is one reason why Islam has a long tradition of arranged marriages, in which parents help their children choose partners. Partly, this may be a historical and cultural legacy. The current western model of love-marriages is itself not a very old one. However, in Muslim societies there are at least two other reasons for maintaining the arranged marriage tradition. First, free mixing between adolescent and adult men and women is discouraged. Originally, this was probably introduced to prevent promiscuity. Scholars think that marriage was not held in especially high esteem by the pre-Islamic Arabs, for whom the basic unit was the tribe. Children stayed with their mother's tribe, so it didn't particularly matter who their father was and sexual intercourse outside of marriage was probably commonplace. Islam, in limiting sexual relations to marriage, was positively affirming that sex is meant to be more than a mere meeting of physical desire. One writer puts it like this: 'Islam does not condemn or deny man's sexual needs but insists that expressions of human sexuality be limited to a particular use under specified conditions: that is, only in the marital state as part of a total mutual commitment and responsibility' (Haneef 1979: 90). Recognising, though, the sheer power of sexual temptation, Muslim tradition tends to keep unrelated men and women apart. Haneef elaborates:

> Islam regards the sexual urge as an extremely powerful element in human nature, one which clamours for free expression if given the slightest encouragement. . . . Recognising the strength of this drive and the fact that it is always present in any situation where men and women interact freely with one another, are alone together, and where bodies are exposed, Islam does not permit any of these things; for it is obviously far more desirable and effective – as well as much more realistic – to prevent temptation than to expect people to resist it when circumstances impel them toward it.
>
> (Haneef 1979: 158)

Muslims living in countries such as the United Kingdom or the United States of America may interpret these traditions more liberally, but many Muslims regard them as quite binding. Haneef's book, for example, describes what Islam says 'about morals, society, government, women and many other matters' and how 'Muslims living in the West practise their religion'. On the other hand, Islam does not see any virtue at all in abstaining from the pleasures of sex and therefore thinks it fair that young people should be helped to find suitable partners as soon as marriage is financially viable. This is the second argument in favour of arranged marriages: if marriage is a religious obligation, and intended to be a blessing, then, even with free mixing between the sexes, it is simply unfair to leave finding a partner to chance or luck. Muslims would point out that while many non-Muslims remain single simply because they cannot find a partner, no Muslim should suffer this fate. Matchmaking is a legitimate concern of the whole community. Perhaps 'assisted marriage' is a better description than 'arranged marriage' (Mercier 1990: 70). Both the man and the woman must consent to marry, and tradition allows a brief meeting before a final decision is made (indeed Muhammad recommended this). Strict rules of consanguinity apply (see *sūrah* 4:22–25) as well as rules about marriage with non-Muslims.

## The ceremony (*nikāḥ*)

Non-Muslim writers often say that marriage in Islam is a civil affair, or a civil contract, *nikāḥ*, not a religious ceremony. This is incorrect. Marriage in Islam falls within the scope of the *sharīʿah*, Islam's divine law which covers all aspects of life and does not distinguish between civil law and canon law. It is, however, correct to say that there is no prescribed form of words that must be used, and that marriage is regarded as a legal or social contract between husband and wife. They contract with each other to enter the mutual duties and responsibilities of spouses either until death intervenes, or until they are legally divorced. Also, while the signing and witnessing of the contract does not have to take place in a mosque, it very often does, but wherever the bride and bridegroom enter their contract, they do so in the sight of God.

To be legally binding under *sharīʿāh*, three conditions must be met. First, a *mahr*, or bridal gift, must be agreed (*sūrah* 4:4). This does not have to be paid in full until a mutually agreed time (upon divorce the full amount must be paid) and always remains the property of the wife. Second, there must be a proposal of marriage. Third, the proposal (*ījāb*) must be accepted (*qubūl*). Both the proposal and acceptance must be witnessed either by two Muslim men, or by one man and two women. Traditionally, brides are represented by their legal guardian, who may be empowered to consent on their behalf. More usually, the guardian's role resembles that of the male relative who 'gives away' during Christian weddings. Islamic Law does not stipulate that the contract has to be written down, although if it is it can include not only arrangements for paying the *mahr* but other 'pre-nuptial agreements'. This might involve the man agreeing not to take any other wives while legally married to his first wife (*sharīʿah* allows polygamy). They may stipulate conditions under which the wife can initiate divorce, normally easier for a man to obtain. While the *sharīʿah* does not prescribe particular words, or say that prayers must be said, conventions have developed covering the marriage contract's legal aspects, and it is also strongly recommended (*mustaḥabb*) that prayers are included.

These conventions vary considerably in different parts of the Muslim world. Where Muslims live in societies where *sharīʿah* is not the law of the land but where mosques are registered as places for the legal solemnising of marriages, whatever 'legal words' the state requires will be incorporated in the *nikāḥ* ceremony. Because local custom varies considerably it is impossible to describe a typical wedding, although what follows here is probably fairly common. The *Sunnah* recommends that *nikāḥ* take place in the context of *'ibādāh*, so it is usual for an *imām* to preside. The *imām* will ask the bride if she consents to the marriage taking place: 'Is it by your own consent that this marriage with . . . takes place', to which the reply is, 'it is by my consent', although she does not have to be in the same room for the contract to be valid. Her guardian may speak on her behalf. If both bride and groom are to be present throughout, it is common for them to kneel in front of the *imām*, clasping each other by the right hand. He may place a handkerchief over their joined hands. In Bangladesh, where I have observed Muslim weddings, this may actually be used to tie their hands together. Traditionally, the ceremony commences with a brief *khuṭbah*, sermon, on the duties and responsibilities of marriage. This will begin with salutations, or blessings, on Allāh and on Muhammad. Following the *Sunnah*, or example of Muhammad himself, several verses from the Qur'ān particularly relevant for the occasion will then be recited, often *sūrah*s 3:102, 4:1 and 33:70–71. The second of these, already cited above, refers directly to marriage as ordained by God so that together husband and wife might find mutual completion in each other. The first and last verses remind bride and bridegroom to fear Allāh (*taqwā*) and to conduct themselves in all things in harmony with his will. In other words, no bad husband or wife can be a good Muslim. Far from being a 'civil affair only', the institution of marriage in Islam is inherently sacred. Next, the *Fātiḥah*, or opening prayer of the Qur'ān (*sūrah* 1), will be recited. This prayer is always said during *ṣalah*:

> In the Name of Allāh, the merciful lord of mercy,
> Praise be to Allāh, Lord of the Creation,
> The merciful lord of mercy,
> King of judgment day [literally, king of the day of religion]
> You alone we worship and to you alone we pray for help,
> Guide us to the straight path.
> The path of those whom you have favoured,
> Not of those who have incurred your wrath,
> Nor of those who have gone astray.

This is followed by the *shahādah* and by the profession of faith, an expanded confession of Muslim belief ('I believe in God, his angels, books, prophets, in the resurrection, and the absolute decree of good and evil'). This is also found in the *Sunnah* (as recorded in the collections known as *aḥadīth*).

Now the legal proceedings are ready to begin, the *ījāb* and *qubūl*, known collectively as *sīghah*, or the *nikāḥ* proper. First the *imām* will invite the bride's guardian to offer her hand to the groom. Assuming that all legal conditions have been satisfied, the guardian may say, 'I betroth to you my daughter (or ward) for a *mahr* of such and such'. The groom will respond, 'With my whole heart and soul, to my marriage with this woman, as well as to the *mahr* settled upon her, I consent. I consent. I consent, and you who are present bear witness to this'. Other forms of words may be used and rings may also be exchanged. Finally, the *imām* will pronounce a blessing: 'O great God, grant that mutual love may reign between this couple as it existed between Adam and Eve, Abraham and Sarah, Joseph and Zalikha, Moses and Zipporah, his highness Muhammad and 'Ayishah, and his highness 'Ali al-Murtaza and Fatimatu 'z-zahrā'. This prayer, invoking the names of the prophets sent by God to proclaim his straight path, and their wives' names, again illustrates that marriage is part of the divine blueprint. Muhammad sometimes used a shorter blessing, 'May Allāh bless you, and may blessing be upon you and may your coming together be auspicious'.

## Festivities

Festivities may precede as well as follow the actual *nikāḥ* ceremony, depending again on local custom. Sometimes, these involve a procession from the groom's house to the bride's house to collect her for the ceremony, or to her new home after the actual *nikāḥ*. Providing the wedding feast (*walīmah*) is the groom's responsibility; Muhammad said, 'The bridegroom will have to give a *walīmah*' (Doi 1984: 140). As it is important to share the joy of childbirth with others, so a wedding is a time for shared joy, especially between the two families involved. The emphasis, too, is on invoking God's blessings, so the feast should be constrained and not too extravagant. Islam discourages overindulgence, since *tawḥīd* implies that 'this-worldly pleasures' should be balanced with activities to feed the soul. Islam's third pillar, *ṣawm*, the obligatory fast during *Ramaḍān*, is a profound annual reminder of this need to balance *dīn* with *dunyā*. The poor as well as the rich should be invited and all guests should be invited by name. According to the *Sunnah*, the feast should not take place until after the marriage has been consummated, without which it still has no legal status.

Historically, some interesting traditions developed, which help illustrate how Islam views the marital union, including sexual intercourse, as wholly within God's blueprint. On their first bedroom encounter, traditionally, the bride should still have her face covered so that the groom can remove the veil himself. Before doing so, saying 'In the name of God', the groom should give her a small gift. This is known as 'the price of uncovering'. Next, he should greet her with the words, 'The night be blessed'. She may reply, 'God bless you'. Then, taking off every piece of her clothing except her undergarment, the groom places her on the bed so that her back faces the *qiblah* (Makkah), the direction in which *ṣalah* (ritual prayer) must always be offered. Before removing the final piece of clothing (which may not be until later that evening), he performs two *rak'ah*s (movements) of prayer.

The whole of this ritual may not be currently practised (the above description was taken from a classic but dated source), although a popular handbook for Muslims, describing a similar custom, says, 'It is recommended that husband and wife pray two *rak'ah*s together before making love' (Al-Kaysi 1986: 122), which shows how prayer and *taqwā* (God-consciousness) belong even in the bedroom. *Ṣalah*, prayer, was a gift from heaven; sex, metaphorically, transports you back there. 'When a worshipper of God marries', said Muhammad, 'he perfects half of his religion' (cited in Robinson 1991: 43). In fact, Muslim writers have not hesitated to use quite erotic language to describe marital bliss, not only as prefiguring the felicity of paradise, but as anticipating ultimate *tawḥīd* (at-one-ness) with God (see Glassé 1991: 357). At the Day of Reckoning (*yawm-ad-dīn*), literally the day of religion), too, souls will be re-united with their bodies. God created everything 'good' (*sūrah* 32:7) including the human body: 'He shaped you and made good your shapes' (*sūrah* 64:3). The Muslim theologian, ibn Arabi (1165–1240), said, 'The most intense and perfect contemplation of God is through women, and the most intense union in the world is the conjugal act'. Jalal ar-Rumi (1207–73), theologian, mystic and poet, said: 'I do not wear a night shirt when I sleep with my beloved' (cited in Glassé 1991: 356).

## A brief comment about divorce in Islam

Islam is both the 'straight path' (see *sūrah* 1:5) and the 'middle way' (*sūrah* 2:143). This means that while it sets a high ideal (that of the perfect man and woman, *al-insān al-kāmil*) and deems people capable of achieving this, it always balances the ideal with pragmatism. It does not place unbearable burdens on people; *sūrah* 2:185 says, 'Allāh desires not hardship for you'. Thus, the ideal marriage is a relationship of mutually enriching harmony and love. However, if an irrevocable breakdown occurs, Islamic Law allows divorce, which is a comparatively simple procedure (albeit usually easier for husbands than for wives). The Qur'ān, though, encourages reconciliation (see *sūrah*s 4:128 and 65:2) and Muhammad himself said, 'of all lawful things, the one which God dislikes most is divorce' (cited in Robinson 1991: 44).

## Dying and death in Islam

Muslims believe in life after death, in the resurrection of the body and in a Day of Reckoning; their extended doctrinal creed, cited above, bears witness to these deeply held convictions. The Qur'ān itself warns that those who rebel against God will be punished, while those who live in harmony with his will have no reason to fear. It also paints word pictures of heaven and of hell. In heaven, the believers will be reunited with their loved ones. Their most prized reward, though, will be fellowship, harmony, *tawḥīd* with God. Pious Muslims know that if they have observed the obligatory duties (Islam's five pillars), if they have lived good, moral lives in conformity with the *sharīʿah*, if they have repented (*tawbah*, turned back to God) whenever they did wrong, God will show them the same mercy he showed Adam at the beginning of time. They know, too, that mere outward observance is valueless unless accompanied by a pure *niyyah* (intent) not to selfishly merit salvation, or to appear pious before others but to worship and serve God for his sake alone. As one Muslim writer put it:

> O My lord, if I worship Thee from fear of Hell,
> burn me in hell,
> If I worship thee from hope of Paradise,
> exclude me thence,
> but if I worship Thee for Thy own sake,
> then withhold not from me Thine Eternal Beauty.
>
> (cited in Mercier 1990: 74)

Muslims also believe that death, like birth, rests in the hands of God: 'Allāh is he who created you and then sustained you, then causeth you to die' (*sūrah* 30:40); 'He . . . has created you from clay, and has decreed a term for you' (*sūrah* 6:2). Since people rarely know when they will die, a Muslim should always be prepared to pass from this world into the next. Muslims believe that the dead will sleep until the resurrection, although a saying of Muhammad has it that two angels come immediately to the grave, and ask, 'What do you say concerning Muhammad'. The tradition continues, 'If the dead person is a true believer he will say, "I testify that he is God's servant and messenger". Then the angels will say to him, "Look at the place which you would have occupied in hell. In exchange God has assigned you a place in heaven"' or vice versa (Robinson 1991: 22). When a Muslim is dying, friends should gather to recite the *shahādah* so that this invocation against the Devil, this attestation that there is no God but God, no will but his, no reality but him, will be the last words heard before death. Just as Muslims are welcomed into the world with God's name, so they are bid farewell. Appropriate verses from the Qur'ān may also be recited, perhaps the 'seven *salāms*' (seven verses containing the Arabic word for 'peace'). Also recommended are *sūrah*s 13 and 36. *Sūrah* 13 promises paradise to those who heed Muhammad's message, who 'persevere in seeking their Lord's countenance and are regular in prayer' (v 22), punishment to those who disbelieve. *Sūrah* 36 contains the significant verse, 'But His command, when He intends a thing, is only that He saith it: Be! and it is' (v 80). This refers to Muslim belief that it was God's *kalām* (word, often identified with the Qur'ān itself) that created the universe. The same *kalām* will command the dead to rise at the resurrection (see also *sūrah* 40:68, 'He it is who quickeneth and giveth death. When He ordains anything, He says unto it: Be! and it is').

## Preparing the body

Traditionally, Muslims are buried on the day they die, preferably before sundown. Often, especially in non-Muslim countries, this will not be possible due to the busy schedules at cemeteries and to legal proceedings, such as the issuing of a death certificate. Muslims are never cremated. Immediately after death, relatives or friends of the same sex as the deceased will undress the corpse and wash it, beginning with the right side. They will repeat this ritual cleansing an odd number of times, usually three or five. This ritual cleansing, known as *ghusl*, always precedes *ṣalah*. It is always important for the body to be clean as well as the soul, especially when preparing for the resurrection. Bodily orifices will be stopped with cotton wool and a white cloth placed over the corpse, including the head. If the deceased is a female, her hair will be plaited and placed behind her back. The corpse will also be perfumed with camphor before being placed in the coffin, on the right side so that when buried the face will lie in the direction of the *qiblah* (Makkah).

There are two circumstances when this ritual is modified. If the person died as a martyr for Islam, they will be buried exactly as they died, without *ghusl*, (only jewellery will be removed). A martyr for Islam will have died during a *jihād*, which is a just or righteous war declared by a legitimate authority in defence of Muslim territory, or sometimes against injustice elsewhere. In the early days of the Muslim empire, or Khalifate (the *Khalīfah*s led the *ummah* after Muhammad's death), a *jihād* could be declared to extend the rule of *sharī'āh* if there was a reasonable chance of success. More recently, Muslims have died as martyrs in Afghanistan, following the Communist take-over and the subsequent ten-year occupation (1979–89) by troops of the former Union of Soviet Socialist Republics. According to the Qur'ān, martyrs go straight to paradise; 'Whosoever fighteth in the way of Allāh, be he slain or be he victorious, on him we shall bestow a vast reward' (*sūrah* 4:74). The second variation is when a person died either on the *ḥajj*, the pilgrimage at Makkah, Islam's fifth pillar, or on the 'lesser pilgrimage', the *'umrah* (the *ḥajj* is obligatory once in a Muslim's lifetime, if financially feasible, and can be performed only during the month of *Dhū'l Ḥijjah*, while the *'umrah* may be performed at any time). Both *ḥajj* and *'umrah* are performed in the state of ritual purity known as *iḥrām* (consecration), when, after bathing and reciting the designated prayers, men dress in two seamless white sheets (women, however, wear their normal clothes). Thus, if Muslims die while in *iḥrām*, they are already ritually clean. The body will still be washed, perhaps just once, but it will then be re-dressed in the same clothes and there is no need to cover the head. Today, so many Muslims perform pilgrimage at Makkah that it is not uncommon for a large number to die in the extreme heat, especially the elderly. Akbar S. Ahmed explains, 'death here is welcome. It is the short cut to paradise. Indeed many old and ailing pilgrims come with this thought in mind. The heat, the crowds, the exertion take a toll on one or two thousand lives during the *ḥajj*' (Ahmed 1991: 145). Here Ahmed is referring to the popular conviction that to die on the *ḥajj*, like dying as a martyr, gains immediate entry into paradise.

## Funeral rite (*janāzah*)

The funeral prayers may take place in the mosque, after one of the canonical *ṣalah* prayers, although here local customs may vary. Sometimes the mosque courtyard is preferred. Relatives and friends should accompany the coffin, reciting the *shahādah en route*. Walking is recommended unless the distance is too far. Before the funeral commences, the mourners will express their *niyyah* (intent) with the usual formula: 'I have purposed to offer up to God only with a sincere heart this prayer'. Next, they will recite the prayer known as the *Subḥān*:

> Holiness to Thee, O God,
> And to Thee be praise,
> Great is Thy name,
> Great is Thy Greatness,
> Great is Thy Praise,
> There is no God but You.

A *takbīr* will then be followed by a *du'ā* (prayer of supplication), which usually invokes blessings on Muhammad, perhaps:

> O God, have mercy on Muhammad and on his descendants, as Thou didst bestow mercy and peace, and blessing and compassion and great kindness upon Abraham and upon his descendants. Thou art praised, and Thou art great. O God, bless Muhammad and his descendants, as Thou didst bless and didst have compassion and kindness upon Abraham and his descendants.

Known as a *Qunūt*, this prayer will be whispered. Other *du'ā*, perhaps prayed spontaneously, may be used. Preceded by another *Allāhu Akbar*, this litany will be repeated two more times. The third *du'ā* will probably be a prayer for the happiness of the departed. After another *takbīr*, all present will then exchange the traditional Muslim greeting of 'Peace be on you' (*As sālamu-'alaykum*) with those on their right and on their left. Sometimes, the mourners will say to the chief mourner, 'It is God's will', to which the traditional reply is, 'I am pleased with God's will'. He may then say, 'There is permission to depart'.

It is considered proper for everyone who took part in the prayers to continue with the procession as far as the graveside. There, the coffin will be lowered into the grave from the rear, with the words, 'In the name of God, by God's grace, and following the *sunnah* of the prophet', or sometimes, 'We commit thee to the earth in the name of God and in the religion of the Prophet'. A qur'ānic formula not dissimilar to words used at Christian committals may also be added: 'From the earth we did create you and into it you shall return, and from it we shall bring you out again' (*sūrah* 20:55), as the grave is filled with soil. Finally, before leaving the grave, the mourners may recite the *Fātiḥah*, which is sometimes repeated at a distance of forty paces from the grave. Tradition says that it is at this point that the two angels, Munkir and Nakir, appear to inform the deceased of their fate. Another old custom was, after three days, to employ several *qāri'* (scholars trained in the art of qur'ānic recitation) to recite the whole of the Qur'ān at the graveside. More than one *qāri'* is needed because normally, under the rules of *tajwīd* (recitation) it takes forty days to read the whole of the Qur'ān, but this can be reduced to as few as three days when divided into 'stages'. Forty days after the burial, relatives and friends may gather to remember the deceased, offering prayers and reading from the Qur'ān.

## Conclusion

In different parts of the Muslim world some of these 'rites of passage' will closely resemble the descriptions given in this chapter. Elsewhere, customs may vary. This is because these 'rites' are not, unlike the obligatory (*farḍ*) prayers, the fast, *zakāt*, the *ḥajj* (and associated feasts), regarded as 'canonical' and so they are not rigidly prescribed in the *sharīʿāh*. Rather, they belong to the area of *ādāb* (propriety, morals), or *ʿādāt* (social custom), which may change from time to time and from place to place. Several of the customs described, though, are derived directly from the *sunnah* of the Prophet, and while this does not render them obligatory, it does render them 'commended' (*mandūb*). Nor must their importance to Muslims be understated. Marking times of joy and sadness, these rites serve to remind Muslims that God's will is absolute in all things. They remind Muslims that his purpose for creating humankind was good. He created humanity 'with truth', he formed and 'shaped good' the human body. If human beings are 'mindful', 'conscious' (*taqwā*) of God in all they do, neither life nor death holds any threat for them. Islam aims, by constantly reminding Muslims that God's will is sovereign, to restore harmony, *tawḥīd*, between the whole creation and its creator. This is why the *shahādah* kept recurring throughout this chapter. Muhammad said, 'I have brought nothing more important than the *shahādah*': through it, humanity sees reality; because of its power, humanity can ultimately return to that Reality. The Qur'ān says that at the End, God will roll the universe back up into himself like a scroll (*sūrah* 22:104). Birth, marriage, death are staging posts on that return journey: Muslims travel towards their goal trusting in God and in God's mercy, praying, 'O Lord! in Thee we put our trust, and unto Thee we turn repentant, and unto thee is the journeying' (*sūrah* 60:4).

### FURTHER READING

*Ahmed, Akbar S. (ed.) (1991) *Discovering Islam: Making Sense of Muslim History and Society*, London, Routledge.

Ally, Mashuq Ibn (1990) 'Second Introductory Paper', *Law, Blasphemy and the Multi-faith Society*, London, Commission for Racial Equality and the Inter-faith Network for the United Kingdom, pp. 21–9.

Cragg, Kenneth C. (1986) *The Call of the Minaret*, (rev. edn), London, Collins.

Doi, Abdur Rahman I. (1984) *Shariah: The Islamic Law*, London, Ta Ha.

*Esposito, John L. (1991) *Islam: The Straight Path* (rev. edn), London, Oxford University Press.

Glassé, Cyril (1991) *The Concise Encyclopaedia of Islam* (2nd edn), London, Stacey International.

Haneef, Suzanne (1979) *What Everyone Should Know About Islam and Muslims*, Lahore, Kazi Publications.

†Hughes, Thomas Patrick (1988) *Dictionary of Islam* (1st edn, 1885), Delhi, Rupa and Co.

‡Al-Kaysi, Narwan Ibrahim (1986) *Morals and Manners in Islam: A Guide to Islamic Adab*, Leicester, The Islamic Foundation.

§Mercier, C.S. (1990) *Skills in Religious Studies Book Three*, London, Heinemann Educational.

**Pickthall, Mohammed Marmaduke (1930) *The Meaning of the Glorious Koran* (1st edn), London, Ta Ha.

**Robinson, Neal (1991) *The Sayings of Muhammad*, London, Duckworth.

*Ruthven, Malise (1991) *Islam in the World*, Harmondsworth, Penguin.

*Schuon, Frithjof (1976) *Understanding Islam*, London, Mandala.

Smith, Wilfred Cantwell (1957) *Islam in Modern History*, Princeton, Princeton University Press.

### *Annotations*

* These are good, introductory texts on Islam. Esposito is a non-Muslim whose writing on Islam generally has Muslim approval. Ahmed is a distinguished Muslim anthropologist. Ruthven's chapter 3, 'The Qur'ānic World View', is especially useful for understanding Islam's theological framework and presuppositions. Schuon is a Muslim philosopher whose book concentrates on Islam's theological dimension.

† This is a classic dictionary of Islam with entries relevant to the theme of this chapter. Although dated, it remains useful. Some recent editions have been revised by Muslim scholars.

‡ This is written as a practical guide on day-to-day life for Muslims. It has entries on birth, marriage and funerals.

§ This was written as a text for lower secondary school students but has excellent, illustrated sections (31 to 37) on rites of passage in Islam.

** These two books contain primary texts, respectively Islam's scripture and some *ḥadīth* of the Prophet, his *sunnah*.

# 5. Judaism

*Alan Unterman*

The ritual framework of Judaism is determined by *halakhah* (law) and *minhag* (custom) which make up traditional Jewish praxis. Neither in *halakhah* nor in *minhag*, however, do we find any terms equivalent to 'a rite of passage'. In other words Torah, the general term for the 'teaching' of both Scripture and the traditions of Rabbinic Judaism, does not distinguish between rituals associated with birth, puberty, marriage and death and other rituals. It is thus artificial to isolate rites of passage rituals from the ritual corpus of Jewish life. The idea of a ritual transition from stage to stage, or from status to status, is referred to in kabbalistic (i.e., mystical) texts which take a 'sacramental' and 'instrumental' view of ritual. From the point of view of *halakhah*, however, the notion of a rite of passage is an external idea, useful though it may be in analysing a religious tradition.

## Birth

According to Jewish teaching, while a child is in its mother's womb a candle burns beside it and an angel teaches it the whole of the Torah. Just before birth the angel touches the child on its lips, and it forgets all it has learnt. This is why a child is born with a cleft upper lip, caused by the fiery angelic finger. Learning God's Torah in this world beyond the womb is, thus, really a process of remembering. The birth of an individual is foreshadowed in the biblical creation story. Adam and Eve are not only the father and mother of all humans, but are also paradigms of every particular man and woman. Adam means 'man' in Hebrew. He was shaped by God from the dust of the earth, and the spirit of the Lord was breathed into him. He is thus a being of the lower world, on a par with the animal kingdom, but he is also made in the image of God and is a partner with God in the work of creation. At death his dust-nature will be returned to the earth from which he was formed while his spirit will return to God. His female companion, Eve, the mother of all life, was formed out of Adam's rib. Although woman was not actually made from the dust, yet she shares the dust-nature of man from whom she was shaped.

In some midrashic and kabbalistic interpretations of the biblical text, Eve is not the first wife of Adam. This is based on the disparity between chapter 1 of Genesis ('male and female created he them') and chapter 2, where God creates Eve specially as a companion for Adam. The first wife was Lilith who was created, together with Adam, but who was unable to stay married to him and fled to the Red Sea. When Adam complained to God, three angels, Sanvi, Sansanvi, and Samangelaf, were sent to bring her back but she refused to go with them. They did, however, manage to extract a promise from her that she will not harm humans when she sees the names of these three angels.

Lilith is jealous of the married state of the descendants of Adam and Eve, and she is particularly jealous of their children. She sleeps with men at night, conceiving demons through their nocturnal emissions, and she attacks women in childbirth and kills new-born babies. Jewish folk traditions prescribe a number of methods for protecting mothers and children against Lilith and her demons. During pregnancy and immediately after birth, holy objects, such as a *sefer torah* (a Torah scroll), or *tefillin* (phylacteries) may be brought into the confinement chamber. An amulet with the names of the angels on it might be hung round the neck of the mother, or placed on the wall. Sometimes a magic circle is drawn round the bed of a woman in labour and the names of the three angels written inside this circle, thus making it out of bounds to Lilith.

In pre-modern times these techniques were taken as seriously as ante-natal and post-natal care are taken today, and in more traditional families there is still considerable reliance on prophylactic measures. Most of these practices, however, are regarded as superstitions by modern Jews. What has remained for them is the recitation of prayers in the synagogue for the welfare of the mother. These prayers exist in two basic rites (and many minor variations).

The Sefardi Rite is of Jews of Iberian origin, most of whom lived in Muslim countries after their expulsion from Spain in 1492, and today it is subscribed to by about half of the Jews in Israel. The Ashkenazi Rite is of Jews of German origin who eventually settled all over central and eastern Europe until modern times, and today Ashkenazim make up the bulk of Jews in western countries.

The Ashkenazi version of this *mi sheberah* ('May he who blessed') prayer is said in Hebrew, and in it the Jewish name of the mother and of her mother are used:

> May he who blessed our ancestors, Abraham, Isaac and Jacob, Moses and Aaron, David and Solomon, may he bless and heal So and So, the daughter of So and So, because her husband commits himself to a donation of such and such to charity on her behalf. In the merit of this deed may the Holy One, blessed be he, be filled with mercy for her to cure and heal, to strengthen and revive her. And may he send her speedily a perfect healing from heaven in all her limbs and nerves, in the midst of the other sick ones of Israel. Now, speedily and soon; and let us say Amen.

## Naming a female child

The births of a female and of a male child are celebrated differently. A girl undergoes a ceremony of name-giving which takes place in the synagogue usually on the next *Shabbat* ('Sabbath day', i.e., Saturday) after her birth. The father is called up for an *aliyah* ('going up') to make a blessing over the reading of the Torah. After the *aliyah* in Ashkenazi communities the following '*mi sheberah*' prayer is said for the mother and daughter and the name of the infant is announced (this time patronymics are used in 'the daughter of' clauses):

> May he who blessed our ancestors, Abraham, Isaac and Jacob, Sarah, Rebecca, Rachel and Leah, may he bless the woman who has given birth So and So, the daughter of So and So, and her infant daughter who was born to her with *mazal tov* ('good luck'). Her name shall be called in Israel So and So the daughter of So and So. Because her husband, and her father, commits himself to a donation of such and such to charity on her behalf, in reward for this deed may her parents merit to raise her to Torah, to the wedding canopy and to good deeds.'

The Jewish name given in this ceremony is the one by which the girl will be known for all religious purposes: it will appear on her wedding certificate, it will be used when '*mi sheberah*' prayers are recited for her recovery from illness or when she gives birth, and it will appear on her tombstone. It is announced ritually so that it has a public role in the community.

Among diaspora Jews today the Jewish name for both boys and girls is often completely different from the secular name. Sometimes there is a similarity of sound or meaning between the two names; thus a girl might be given the Jewish name Faige (from the Yiddish 'feigel' meaning 'a bird') and the similar sounding, but totally different, secular name Phoebe (from a Greek word meaning 'to shine'). Sometimes the secular name is a translation of the Jewish name into the vernacular. Thus Shoshanah might be known as Rose, although a better translation of this Hebrew word would be 'lily'.

## Circumcision (*berit milah*, literally 'covenant of circumcision')

A newly born boy should undergo circumcision on the eighth day after birth, even if that day is a *shabbat* or festival. The operation cannot take place before the eighth day but it may be delayed if there are medical grounds. Jaundice is one of the most common reasons for delayed circumcision because the *mohel* ('circumciser') will not operate unless the colour of the baby's skin is normal. If the ceremony is delayed, however, as soon as the child is fit the operation should take place on the next available weekday.

When two sibling children, or two first cousins, have died after circumcision, a third child would not be circumcised until he had grown up and become strong. Obviously haemophilia or some other medical condition might make circumcision impossible, in which case the child is considered as if already circumcised. If the child is born without a foreskin then a drop of blood ('the blood of the Covenant') must be removed from the penis as an act of symbolic circumcision. The same is the case with adult male converts to Judaism who need to undergo circumcision as part of the process of conversion. Some of them may have been circumcised by a doctor as youngsters and they need to undergo symbolic circumcision when they become 'children of the Covenant'.

On the first Friday night after the birth of a boy, and in some communities on the night before the circumcision, family and friends gather at the parents' house to eat chick peas and drink beer. This ceremony is known as a *shalom zachar* (literally 'peace of the male'). This party has been understood as a mourning meal for the Torah the child had learnt in the womb and had now forgotten. Chick peas and other round foods are typical of a mourners' meal, and this gathering at the parents' home is like the custom of gathering at the house of mourners to comfort them.

The night before the circumcision is a time for guarding the child against the predatory evil spirits which seek to harm him. It is known as a 'night of guarding' or *vach-nacht* ('watch night') in Yiddish. There are a number of customs, the purpose of which is to protect the child from demons and from danger on the morrow. Thus, for instance, people stay awake all night studying Torah in the house of circumcision, preferably in the presence of a *minyan* ('number', i.e., a quorum of ten men). The Polish custom, still practised among some Ashkenazi Jews, is to bring a class of youngsters from the *heder* ('room', i.e., religion school) to the house to recite prayers. The sound of innocent little children at prayer was powerful enough to undermine even the most persistent demons. The circumcision knife might be placed under the pillow in the mother's bed and the father may recite sections from the kabbalistic classic, the *Zohar*, which are thought to have prophylactic power. In Israel, hospitals usually have a special room for circumcisions, but in the diaspora the ceremony most often takes place in the home. It is customary to light candles in the room where the operation will take place and to gather together a *minyan* of ten adult males. It is not customary, however, to invite people to the circumcision ceremony because it is a religious ceremony. Once invited, people would have to attend since they would not be able to refuse participation in a *mitzvah* ('commandment', i.e., religious obligation). Instead, the parents merely inform people that the circumcision will take place at a certain time on a particular date. This is considered information and not an invitation.

Someone is chosen by the parents to hold the baby on his lap during the operation. He is known as a *sandak* (or more commonly *sandek*), a word of Greek origin meaning a patron or co-father. A grandfather, the rabbi of the community, or the father himself usually fills the role of *sandak*, but it can go to any adult male. It is not customary among Ashkenazim for a woman to hold the baby during circumcision, but this does happen in some Sefardi communities. The child is brought from its mother to the circumcision room by a married female, specially chosen for this role. She hands the baby to her husband at the door of the room. The man and the woman are known among Yiddish speakers as *kevater* and *kevaterin* respectively. These terms are from the Germanic root *gevatter*, meaning a godfather. The *sandek*, too, is thought of as a godfather who, together with the *kevater*s, will be responsible for helping the child in later life. Acting as *kevater*s is supposed to be a *segulah* ('a magical potency') for a barren couple, helping them to have children of their own.

When the *kevater* brings the child in, the assembled family and friends greet it with the words: '*barukh haba*!' ('Blessed be he that comes'). The child's father declares that he has appointed the *mohel* to circumcise his child, though in ancient times it was the father who performed the operation himself. The *mohel*, or the father, takes the child from the *kevater* and places him momentarily on an empty chair, set up beside the chair where the *sandek* is sitting. This empty chair is for the prophet Elijah, known as 'the angel of the Covenant' (Mal. 3:1), who attends every circumcision because he complained to God that the people of Israel were neglecting the Covenant. He is thus forced to return to earth to witness every occasion when Jews re-affirm the Covenant, and to act as a heavenly guardian to the child. Some scholars understand the greeting '*barukh haba*!' to be words of welcome to Elijah who enters the room with the child. By placing the baby on Elijah's chair, it is thus placed on Elijah's lap immediately prior to the operation. In some communities an elaborately carved chair of Elijah is brought to the place of the circumcision for the invisible angelic guest to sit on. All those assembled stand during the ritual except for the *sandek* (and Elijah of course).

As the child is placed on the empty chair the *mohel* declares: 'This is the throne of Elijah the prophet, may he be remembered for good.' He then recites several verses from the Bible, mostly from the Book of Psalms, and addresses Elijah thus: 'Elijah, angel of the Covenant, behold your place is before you, remain on my right side and support me'. While the *sandek* holds the child on his knees, keeping its legs open, the *mohel* cleans the penis with disinfectant, makes a blessing and then cuts off the foreskin. He then tears back the membrane covering the penis and sucks out blood from the wound, either with his mouth (the practice of pre-modern times) or with a glass pipette (a modern innovation to avoid the transference of germs). The actual operation takes only a few seconds, so the father immediately makes his blessing: 'Blessed are You O Lord our God, King of the Universe, who has sanctified us with his commandments and commanded us to bring him in into the Covenant of our father Abraham'. Everyone in the room responds with the words: 'Just as he has entered the Covenant so may he enter into Torah, the wedding canopy and good deeds'.

The foreskin that has been cut off is placed in a container of earth or sand. A bandage is then placed on the penis, the baby is dressed, and he is handed to someone appointed by the family to hold him for the name-giving ceremony.

## Naming of a male child

During the naming ceremony a cup of wine is held by the *mohel* or rabbi as he recites two blessings followed by the naming formula. During the recital of the latter some drops of wine are placed into the mouth of the baby. The naming formula is as follows:

> Our God and God of our fathers preserve this child to his father and to his mother, and let his name be called in Israel So and So, the son of So and So (his father's name). May the father (or if deceased 'the father in Paradise') rejoice in the one who has gone out from his loins and may the mother (or 'the mother in Paradise') be glad in the fruit of her womb. [various biblical verses follow, including] It is written: 'And I said unto you: In your blood you shall live.' [At this point wine is placed in the baby's mouth.] May this little child So and So, the son of So and So, become great. Just as he has entered the Covenant so may he enter into the study of Torah, into the wedding canopy and into good deeds. Amen.

The *mohel* recites prayers for the spiritual welfare of the baby, which depict the circumcision as a sacrificial offering before the throne of glory. He asks for the angels on high to give the child a holy and pure soul with which to comprehend and keep God's teachings. He then prays for the baby's full recovery from the operation using the standard '*mi sheberah*' formula. A meal or light repast follows the ceremony. If a child dies before being circumcised then his foreskin is removed just before burial and he is given a Hebrew name. If a baby girl dies before being given a name then she too is named prior to burial. This naming is to ensure that God will have mercy on the child, and at the messianic resurrection of the dead the child will have a Jewish identity.

The custom today among Ashkenazim is for the mother to have the right to choose the name for her first child, usually calling him or her after a deceased close relative, particularly a parent. Until modern times the custom used to be for the father to have the right to name the first-born and the mother to have the right to call the second child after one of her relatives. Even today, if the father dies before the circumcision of his child then a male child would be given his father's name. Since it is customary to name children after relatives, the same first names tend to recur in families. Ashkenazi Jews do not call a child by the same name as a close living relative. This is based on the folk belief that if the angel of death comes looking for the older relative it might kill the younger relative with a similar name by mistake. Sefardi Jews do not subscribe to this folk prohibition and do indeed call their children by the same name as living parents, grandparents, uncles, aunts etc. There is ample evidence from Jewish literature that the Sefardi custom better represents ancient practice. In talmudic times children were called after living relatives and sons were called by the same name as their father while he was still alive.

It is believed that the Jewish name parents choose for their child is actually put into their mouths by God Himself. This name is already the heavenly name of the child, engraved on the Throne of Glory, and it is a holy name representing the inner personality of its bearer. This explains why, in Jewish literature, there are many attempts to associate the names of biblical characters with their personalities and biographies. At the end of the *Amidah*, the central prayer of the liturgy, some people have the custom of reciting a verse from the Bible which begins with the first letter of their name and ends with the last letter. Through this association of their name with God's teaching, they prevent the forces of evil from taking the name into exile, and their name (symbolising the divine element in each Jew) therefore remains holy. It further ensures that the Torah will save them from *gehinnom* ('purgatory') after death and their name will be remembered at the resurrection of the dead. It is even recommended by one authority that the verse should be recited by the name-bearer before any important undertaking.

It is the sanctity of the name which also lies behind the custom of giving boys their name only after their foreskin has been removed, and they have thus entered the Covenant. It is even customary for the parents, before the circumcision, to refuse to tell people the name they have chosen for their son. This prevents anyone casting an evil eye on the child, which is still in a vulnerable spiritual condition until the circumcision. A leading seventeenth-century kabbalist, Abraham Azulai, explained the mystical significance of the naming ceremony as follows:

> A man is not called by the name of man except through the commandment of circumcision. Without it he is called a demon and not a man. As long as the demonic forces have a hold on a man, through the foreskin and the uncleanliness of man, it is impossible for the higher soul (which distinguishes him as a Jew) to alight upon him and it is impossible for him to be called by the name of an Israelite. Thus it is customary not to give him a name until after the circumcision, when the foreskin and uncleanliness have already gone. Then the secret of the higher soul rests on him and he may be called an Israelite man through the commandment of circumcision.
>
> (Chesed Le-Avraham 2:52)

This kabbalistic view, that circumcision is a rite of passage which inaugurates an individual into the community of Israel, is not, in fact, in accord with the *halakhah* which takes a less mystical view of the matter. According to the *halakhah*, a child born to a Jewish mother is already an Israelite by the biological fact of birth. Of course he needs circumcision, but if his parents do not circumcise him he is still a Jew. Indeed, there is a reference in one medieval text (*Sefer Chasidim*) to a custom of calling a child by his Hebrew name as soon as he is placed in his cradle, i.e., before his circumcision, and placing a copy of the Book of Leviticus under his head to indicate his spiritual identity as a Jew.

The name of a sick person may be changed so that the heavenly decree against the person with the previous name will not apply to the new name. The additional name is usually one which means 'life' or 'healing'. If the sick person recovers, from then on the person and his children, who are known as son or daughter of So and So, would use the new name first, followed by the old name. If, however, the change of name did not improve the person's health, then after the death, his or her children would use the old name first, followed by the new name. The reason why a new name is added to the old name, rather than changing the name entirely, is because a number of mystics insisted that the name given to a person at birth is the name which is used in heaven and thus represents the very essence of a person. To change it entirely might harm the person's life-force, except in the case of a great saint whose life is itself focused on God, or if the name is changed by a God-fearing sage who is able to call down a completely new soul on the person. Sin can cause people's names to diminish so that when they die and the angel of death asks them their name they are unable to answer because some letters of their name have simply slipped away.

## *Bar mitzvah* and *bat mitzvah*

In Jewish law adulthood is achieved by boys and girls when puberty begins and the sign of this is the growth of two pubic hairs. The examination of individuals to ascertain whether they have pubic hairs or not is obviously problematic, not least because pubic hairs may have grown and fallen out. The ages of twelve years for girls and thirteen years for boys were therefore fixed upon as the average ages of puberty and adulthood. At these ages girls and boys become *bat mitzvah* and *bar mitzvah* respectively, and boys may now be counted as one of the ten men who make up a *minyan* for prayer.

These ages have remained the accepted approximation for adulthood, but where the *halakhah* insists that only a true adult is needed they are not sufficient. Thus a *bar mitzvah* boy would not be allowed to read from the Torah on some special occasions, or be responsible for baking the unleavened bread for Pesach unless he had pubic hair, or his beard hair had grown. Since the middle ages it has been customary for the community to celebrate the coming of age of a male child in a *bar mitzvah* ceremony. The term '*bar mitzvah*' ('son of the commandment'), and its female equivalent '*bat mitzvah*' ('daughter of the commandment'), indicate that the young adult is now subject to the commandments. According to the *Zohar*, the main mystical text of Judaism, from the age of thirteen the boy inherits a new soul from God, and two angels begin to accompany him. They will be his constant companions for the rest of his life, signifying his good and evil inclinations.

The form which a *bar mitzvah* ceremony takes is for the boy to be called up for an *aliyah* to recite a blessing over a section of the *sidra*, or weekly Torah reading. The main Torah reading takes place on *Shabbat* morning, with smaller readings on *Shabbat* afternoons, and Mondays and Thursdays. In pre-modern times it was quite usual for the *bar mitzvah* boy to be called up on a Monday or Thursday, as it was impossible for everyone to have an *aliyah* on a Saturday morning. The practice today is to have the main *bar mitzvah* ceremony on *Shabbat*. The minimum that is expected of a *bar mitzvah* boy is the singing of the blessings before and after the Torah portion: 'Bless the blessed Lord'. The congregation respond: 'Blessed be the Lord who is blessed for ever and ever'. The boy continues: 'Blessed are you, Lord our God, King of the Universe, who has chosen us from all the peoples and given us his Torah. Blessed are you, Lord, who gives the Torah'. After the portion the boy continues: 'Blessed are you, Lord our God, King of the Universe, who has given us a Torah of truth, and planted eternal life in our midst. Blessed are you, Lord, who gives the Torah.' The section from the Torah may be read for the boy by the regular Torah reader. The *bar mitzvah*, however, can also read a section of the Torah, or the concluding section (*maftir*) of the Torah and the *haftarah* portion from the prophets which follows it. In the maximal case he may even read the whole *sidra* plus the *haftarah*. It can take around a year of special tuition for the boy to learn how to read the text and sing it to the liturgical tune.

The day of a boy's *bar mitzvah* is a testing time for him, when he will stand in front of the whole congregation. Apart from the Torah reading, the boy will usually also be expected to make a speech at the *bar mitzvah* party. In many Orthodox families it is taken for granted that the boy will do all the Torah reading. The real ordeal for him is to learn a subtle discourse on some obscure subject, written for him by his rabbi, which shows his attainments in the study of the Talmud.

What is common to all forms of *bar mitzvah* is the element of trial by ordeal, proving the worthiness of the boy to be an adult and to become a full member of the community. To the boy it conveys a sense of achievement and indeed matures him. The pain of preparation and of performance, however, is ameliorated by the presents which family and guests bring him. As the Jewish home has become more secularised in modern times so the ritual of *bar mitzvah* has become more important. In the past the *bar mitzvah* was the beginning of the serious ritual involvement of the child in Jewish life. Today it is often the last element of serious ritual involvement before the estrangement from religion which will characterise the boy's teenage years.

For the parents and the wider family the *bar mitzvah* represents a milestone, since the boy's last religious celebration was his circumcision. The family will host relatives and friends to a party to commemorate the boy's coming of age, and the *Zohar* actually compares such a party to a wedding feast. Indeed, it is a very emotional time, with grandparents often still alive who may not survive to see the wedding ceremony. The mother sees her son move from spiritual dependency to independence and the father customarily makes a benediction after his son has been called up: 'Blessed be he who has freed me from responsibility for this child'. The rabbi's sermon on the *Shabbat* morning of a *bar mitzvah* will usually contain a special message for the boy and perhaps also some mention of the contribution of his parents and grandparents to the life of the community. At the end of the sermon in many communities the rabbi blesses the boy with the words of the biblical priestly blessing: 'May the Lord bless you and keep you. May he shine his face on you and be gracious to you. May he lift his countenance to you and grant you peace. Amen'.

Just prior to his thirteenth Hebrew birthday the boy will begin to put on *tefillin* (phylacteries) every weekday morning for prayers. These consist of two blackened leather boxes, bound to the left arm and head with black leather straps. Inside the boxes are biblical paragraphs handwritten on parchment. In many Ashkenazi communities the boy begins to put on *tefillin* up to a month before his birthday. In Sefardi communities, however, he does not put them on until his actual thirteenth birthday, and this day is celebrated by the family and guests. Those in synagogue are invited to a party after morning prayers.

A boy's thirteenth Hebrew birthday does not fall on the date of his thirteenth secular birthday because the Jewish ritual year is a lunar year of twelve months, considerably shorter than the solar year. Seven times every nineteen years an extra month is intercalated into the Jewish year to bring the two back together. This extra month, known as the Second *Adar*, leads to an anomaly concerning *bar mitzvah* boys. Suppose two boys are born in a leap year, the older one say on 25 First *Adar* and the younger one on 3 Second *Adar*. If their thirteenth year is not a leap year then the younger boy will be *bar mitzvah* first (on 3 *Adar*) and the older boy will be *bar mitzvah* three weeks later (on 25 *Adar*). One reason which is proffered in explanation is that spiritual maturity always follows the Hebrew calendar.

### *BAT MITZVAH*

Although the coming of age of a girl, at twelve years, is as well established in *halakhah* as the boy's *bar mitzvah*, it receives far less attention in traditional communities. The main reason for this is that a woman's religious role is less public than that of a man. She does not lead the prayers, is not counted as a member of a *minyan* quorum, is not called up for an *aliyah* to recite blessings over the Torah, and does not have to put on *tefillin*. Her coming of age, which sees the onset of menstruation and the ability to bear children, is therefore a more private matter. Among Reform Jews a much greater public role is assigned to a woman and there is no religious activity from which she is excluded, including acting as rabbi or cantor. In the nineteenth century a confirmation ceremony was introduced by German Reform congregations for boys and girls around the age of sixteen, when they could understand more about their religion. This was meant to replace the *bar mitzvah* for boys and to provide an equivalent ceremony for girls. Confirmation is still practised in some USA Reform communities, but as it was borrowed from the Christian church, it never caught on sufficiently to displace the *bar mitzvah*. A *bat mitzvah* ceremony was therefore introduced for girls to parallel the *bar mitzvah* ceremony for boys. This was eventually adopted even by modern Orthodox synagogues.

The main difference between Orthodox and non-Orthodox *bat mitzvah* ceremonies lies in how closely the activities of the *bat mitzvah* girl imitate those of the boy in the *bar mitzvah*. In Reform and Conservative ceremonies girls prepare a Torah reading or *haftarah* reading, and are called up just like a boy. In Orthodox ceremonies the girl is never called up in a normal congregational service. Some Orthodox feminist groups, however, have started experimental *bat mitzvah* ceremonies attended only by women, where the *bat mitzvah* girl reads a portion from the Torah. It is more usual for a group of girls to be *bat mitzvah* together in an Orthodox synagogue on a Sunday, some time after their twelfth Hebrew birthday. They will prepare readings on a theme in Hebrew and English which they will present, accompanied by special prayers and a sermon. The parents host a reception or party afterwards to celebrate the coming of age of their daughters and their responsibility to keep the *mitzvot*. The earliest Orthodox support for *bat mitzvah* ceremonies was found among German rabbis who sought to combat the attractiveness of Reform. Even modified forms of the ceremony, however, have been condemned by ultra-Orthodox rabbis who see in it a concession to Reform, or an imitation of Christian practices. They claim that such a celebration involves too much of a change in the traditional status of women and that it has no precedent in the past. They even regard the festive meal, to which family and friends are invited, as without religious significance. Several halakhic authorities have prohibited the use of synagogues for *bat mitzvah* ceremonies on the grounds that holy places should not be used for purely secular purposes. In Israel Orthodox *bat mitzvah* ceremonies do not take place in synagogues. Instead, the father of the girl is usually called up for an *aliyah* on the *Shabbat* after her twelfth birthday. She may then have a party at her home for her girlfriends.

## Marriage

Adam was created alone, without a companion, unlike all the other animals which were created in pairs. God realised that being alone was not good for Adam so he brought all the animals to him to see if he could find a partner, but they were unsuitable as companions. Adam managed to give each one a name, i.e., he comprehended its nature, but he found neither sexual fulfilment nor real relationship with them. So God put Adam into a deep sleep and took out one of his ribs which he then shaped into another human being, Eve, who became Adam's companion. According to a view found in rabbinic and mystical literature, it was not a rib that was removed from the first man, but God actually split Adam down the middle. Till then he had been an hermaphrodite, half-male and half-female, with the two halves joined back to back. That is why, at the beginning of Genesis, it states, 'And God created Adam in his own image, in the image of God created he him, male and female created he them' (Gen. 1:27). In the operation God thus separated the man and woman and presented Adam with the other half of himself, to whom he could now relate. On seeing Eve he said, 'Bone of my bone and flesh of my flesh' (Gen. 2:23). The Torah concludes this story with the words: 'Therefore a man shall leave his father and his mother and cleave to his wife, and they shall become as one flesh'.

This context helps to explain the oft reiterated idea that unmarried people are not really complete, and until they have found, and married, a member of the opposite sex they have not found the other half of themselves. Thus it is said that the reason there is a reference to the creation of man in the seven wedding benedictions is precisely to teach this lesson that the birth of a person is always an incomplete thing. Until a man and a woman stand under the wedding canopy they are not yet properly born. Indeed, the canopy (*huppah*) in a sense symbolises the womb, for when the couple step out of it they are said to be born anew and all their sins are forgiven them. The day before their wedding is thus a fast day for bride and groom, modelled on the fast of the Day of Atonement, which is meant to call up God's forgiveness of sins.

The Jewish ideal is for a young man and a young woman to marry early, to 'build a faithful house in Israel' and to have as many children as God blesses them with. In traditional communities the sexes do not mix freely before marriage so there is little opportunity of a girl and a boy meeting and falling in love. It is a duty of parents to enable their children to marry and in the case of orphans or of paupers the community has to take responsibility for this. Most traditional marriages are arranged either by a relative, a family friend or a professional marriage broker (*shadchan*) and an arranged marriage is known as a *shidduh*. Once children are in their late teens their parents will expect them to meet members of the opposite sex on a *shidduh* with a view to finding a marriage partner. The potential partner having been pre-selected by the amateur or professional matchmaker, there is no need for long courtships before the couple make up their mind. After the initial introduction, three or four meetings are usually sufficient for them to decide in principle whether they wish to marry or whether they are not suitable for each other. There is no secular engagement party among traditionalists. Instead, they may have a *tenaim* ('conditions') ceremony which takes place in a private home. There, a document of commitment to proceed with the marriage is signed on behalf of both families. Since this document is considered by many communities as absolutely binding, and not to be broken, they prefer not to put the engagement in writing. They still have a ceremony in a private house but it is accompanied with only a verbal agreement to marry, known in Yiddish as a '*vort*' ('word').

## The wedding ceremony

A day or two before the wedding ceremony, the bride goes to the *mikveh* (ritual bath) for the first time. She will usually be accompanied by women relatives, and among Sefardi communities her visit is turned into a celebration for the community womenfolk. The *mikveh* is a pool of 'living water' made up from rain water, or other natural water source, and kept in a tank. Ordinary tap water fills a large adjacent bath which is in contact with the contents of the *mikveh*. This contact transforms the tap water into 'living water'. Women totally immerse themselves in the transformed tap water a week after their menstrual period has ceased, before resuming sexual relations with their husbands, or, as in the case of the bride, before their first sexual encounter.

In strictly Orthodox families the wedding date will be arranged so as to fall shortly after the end of the seven clean days following the bride's menstrual period. During these days a woman has to examine herself with a cloth placed in the vagina to see if there are any bloodstains, indicating that the menstrual period has not quite finished. If it is feared that the bride will still be ritually unclean at the time of the wedding ceremony she may take a pill that delays the onset of her period. Among Ashkenazim there is a custom for a bride and groom not to see each other for the week before the wedding, but the Sefardim impose no such restriction on the couple.

On the *Shabbat* before the wedding the groom is called up for an *aliyah*, known in Yiddish as an *aufruff*, in his home synagogue. He is greeted with traditional songs, and, among Oriental Jews, women shriek with joy and throw sweets at him. After the service the groom's family usually host a *kiddush* in honour of the forthcoming wedding.

On the wedding day the bride and groom will not be left alone, because demons are likely to harm them if they are on their own. It is customary for them to fast from dawn till after the wedding ceremony and to recite the confession of sins in their prayers. This day is a kind of private Day of Atonement for them. When they leave the *huppah* ('wedding canopy') all their sins are forgiven them and they are like newborn children. The wedding canopy consists of an embroidered piece of cloth supported by four posts, symbolising the house of the groom. It can also be a simple prayer shawl (*tallit*) held up by four men.

It is customary for the wedding to take place in the bride's community, often inside the synagogue, as practised by modern Orthodox Ashkenazim, by most Sefardim, and by Conservative and Reform Jews. More traditional Ashkenazim prefer to set up the *huppah* under the open sky, as the stars are a symbol of fertility. A number of rabbis have objected to synagogue weddings, particularly with organ accompaniment, as imitation of Christian customs.

The wedding document (*ketubah*) is in Aramaic, a sister-language to Hebrew and the lingua franca of the Middle East during the early centuries of the Common Era. The rabbi writes the Jewish date, the Hebrew names and patronymics of bride and groom, and the location of the marriage, all in Hebrew characters in the printed *ketubah* text. The *ketubah* is duly signed by two witnesses who must be adult male Jews who are not close kin of either bride or groom. The *ketubah* guarantees the wife financial support should the husband divorce her, or predecease her. It also establishes the bona fides of the marriage, and if it takes place under Orthodox auspices it will serve as sufficient proof of the Jewish status of both parties for Orthodoxy.

Among Ashkenazim the groom goes to the bride's room to cover the face of the bride with a veil, a ceremony known in Yiddish as *bedeken*. The biblical patriarch Jacob married the wrong girl because his father-in-law tricked him and he did not view the face of his bride beforehand (Gen. 29:21–25). Even today, in certain Orthodox communities, the bride wears a thick veil under the *huppah* which completely masks her face.

The groom returns to the *huppah* accompanied by his best man, whose duty it is to guard him, and by members of his family. He stands facing towards Jerusalem, the holiest place for Jews. If the wedding is in the synagogue, then he will have his back to the congregation. The bride walks to the canopy either on her father's arm, between her parents or between the two mothers. The mothers may hold plaited candles alight in their hands as they accompany her. She either goes directly to stand at the groom's right side or she circumambulates him three or seven times, depending on the custom, before taking up her place beside him. As she does so, the cantor sings the *mi adir* prayer:

> He who is mighty [*mi adir*] above all things, he who is blessed above all things, he who is great above all things, may he bless the groom and the bride.

The rabbi in charge of the ceremony then addresses the couple. He usually exhorts them to keep the traditions of Jewish married life (e.g., the kosher food laws, hospitality, the use of the *mikveh*, or the rituals of *Shabbat* and festivals) and to follow the example of their parents and grandparents. After the sermon he takes a silver cup full to the brim with sweet red wine and recites two blessings over it. The first is the blessing over wine and the second is the betrothal blessing:

> Blessed are you, Lord our God King of the Universe, who has sanctified us with his commandments and commanded us concerning forbidden sexual relationships. Who has prohibited to us those who are merely betrothed and has permitted to us those who have been married to us, through the ritual of *huppah* and sanctification. Blessed are you, Lord, who sanctifies his people Israel through *huppah* and sanctification.

The rabbi passes the goblet of wine to the parents, who stand beside the groom and bride under the *huppah*, to give their children some wine to drink. The groom then takes the wedding ring. This must be a plain band of precious metal, for if it contained any jewels the bride might be misled as to its real value. The rabbi asks the groom if it indeed belongs to him, and then he shows it to the two witnesses who satisfy themselves that it is of the requisite minimum value.

Holding the ring above the bride's right forefinger, the groom makes a Hebrew declaration, usually repeating the words after the rabbi and cantor:

> Behold you are sanctified to me [*li*] with this ring according to the law of Moses and Israel.

He then places the ring on her finger and if she accepts it then she accepts him as her spouse. The reason why the rabbi and cantor both prompt the groom, with the cantor saying the word '*li*', is so that the congregation should not think that the rabbi himself was betrothing the bride.

The *ketubah* is then read aloud in Aramaic, and sometimes a precis of it is also read in the vernacular, to serve as a break between the two parts of the wedding ceremony: the *erusin*, or betrothal, and the *nissuin*, or marriage proper. In ancient times the two parts were completely separate, with as much as a year elapsing between the giving of the ring and the recital of the seven benedictions under the *huppah*. Once the two parts were united into one ceremony it became customary to make a break between them with the *ketubah* reading, to show that they are indeed different rituals.

The *ketubah* is the property of the bride and it is handed to her after it is read. The cantor then takes the second cup of wine and sings the seven *nissuin* blessings over it. These blessings deal with the creation of man in God's image and the creation of woman from him, how Zion rejoices in her children, and God gives joy to the bride and groom. It ends with the longest of the seven blessings:

> Blessed are you, Lord our God King of the Universe, who has created happiness and joy, groom and bride, rejoicing and song, gladness and merriment, love and brotherhood, peace and companionship. Speedily, O Lord our God, may there be heard in the cities of Judah and in the public places of Jerusalem the sound of happiness and joy, the voice of the groom and the voice of the bride, the jubilant sound of grooms from their canopies and youths from their feasts of song. Blessed are you, Lord, who rejoices the groom with the bride.

One parent from each side gives the groom and bride wine to drink from the wedding cup. A glass wrapped in cloth or paper is then placed before the groom who smashes it by stamping on it with his right foot. This element of destruction in the midst of joy is to remember the destruction of Jerusalem, in line with the words of Psalm 137: 'If I forget thee, O Jerusalem . . . if I put not Jerusalem above my chief joy'. Reference to this Psalm is also given as the reason behind the custom of smearing ash on the groom's forehead immediately prior to the wedding, ash being a sign of mourning for Jerusalem.

Jewish folklore has interpreted the breaking of the glass by the groom in a number of different ways. It is thought of as symbolic of the breaking of the hymen of a virgin bride. According to the kabbalists, it is an offering to the powers of evil, either to placate them so that they do no harm, or to prevent the evil eye emanating from one of the guests from harming the couple. It is said that if the groom is unable to break the glass at the first attempt this means the bride will be the dominant character in the home.

At the end of the ceremony the rabbi blesses the couple with the words of the biblical priestly blessing. Among Ashkenazim the wedding ceremony ends with the couple being taken to an empty room, to spend some time alone together and to break their fast. This is known as *yihud*, and is witnessed by two witnesses. The bride and groom have to spend a few minutes together, sufficient time in theory actually to consummate the marriage. Since an unrelated boy and girl cannot be left alone without a chaperone, this *yihud* is a recognition by the community that they are now married. Most Sefardi communities do not have a specific act of *yihud* immediately after the wedding ceremony.

It is customary to have a party after the wedding ceremony, at the end of which the seven marriage blessings are recited immediately after the grace after meals. For the next week a smaller party is held every evening, hosted by family or friends, to entertain the couple with food, music and song. At these the seven blessings are recited if a *minyan* is present and there is a 'new face' who was not at the wedding or at any of the previous parties for this couple. The only day on which a 'new face' is not needed to recite the seven blessings is *Shabbat*, since the Sabbath day itself is considered a 'new face' guest.

## Divorce

Jewish marriage is a religious bond which can only be dissolved by either the death of one partner or a religious divorce. In the latter case the husband has a document (*get*) written for him and his wife in a religious law court (*bet din*) by a scribe. The *get* is witnessed by two witnesses. He must then deliver the *get* to his wife of his own free will, either directly or via a third party, again in the presence of two witnesses. Among Ashkenazim the woman must accept the *get* of her own free will, and thus if either party refuses to participate in the divorce it has no validity.

Originally Jews practised polygamy, but this was prohibited to Ashkenazim in the middle ages. In theory, at least, polygamy is still possible for non-Ashkenazi Jews, although it is prohibited in the modern state of Israel. Since it was the rabbis who prohibited polygamy, if an Ashkenazi husband can gain the agreement of one hundred rabbis then he can marry a second time, even if his first wife refuses to accept a *get*. A wife remains a 'chained woman' (*agunah*) if she cannot obtain a divorce. The most difficult case of an *agunah* is where the husband has disappeared and it is not known whether he is alive or dead.

Although the husband must divorce his wife freely, a *bet din* may pressurise him to do so if they find that by law he ought to divorce her, e.g., if he has mistreated her, or he is impotent. In ancient times he was even beaten until he said: 'I am willing [to give a *get*]'. The great medieval halakhist, Maimonides, explained this contradiction as follows. Every believing Jew really wishes to follow the dictates of God's law, and it is only the evil inclination in the husband that prevents him agreeing to give the *get*. The beating thus does not affect his free will but only overcomes his evil inclination. So when he declares, 'I am willing', that is a genuine reflection of his inner will. In Israel there are a number of husbands who have spent years in prison but still refuse to divorce their wives and win their release.

## Conversion

The most fundamental rite of passage takes place when a Gentile changes his or her religious status and converts to Judaism. Converts are literally considered as if they were newly born, having no biological family members. Their new father and mother are the biblical figures Abraham and Sarah, who first began to convert people to monotheism some four thousand years ago. Kabbalists view converts as people who have been given a new soul, or who have been born with a Jewish soul in a Gentile body, which led them to undertake the spiritual journey to Judaism in the first place.

Conversion has to take place in front of a *bet din* of three judges (sing. *dayan*, pl. *dayanim*) who will open a file on a would-be convert. The Talmud recommends that one should discourage converts while at the same time bringing them near, and so the *bet din* will initially try to discourage the would-be convert. If the *dayan* who interviews candidates is convinced that they are serious and determined, he will assign them a teacher. While studying, converts will be assigned a family to spend *Shabbat* and festivals with, and to learn about the dietary laws in a practical way.

A course of study for conversion may last for several years in the diaspora, although it tends to be shorter in Israel. It will usually involve both converts and their future Jewish spouses, and at the end of it converts must be willing to accept the whole Torah, without reservations. When the teacher concludes that a convert is ready, the *bet din* will be informed. They will consider the teacher's reports, interview the candidate, and if satisfied they will arrange for the conversion to take place. Many people drop out of the conversion procedure in the initial stages when they realise how much there is to learn about Judaism and how long it takes.

The actual process of conversion involves circumcision for the male, and immersion in the *mikveh* for both male and female converts in front of three *dayanim*. Once converted, the convert has to keep all the laws of the *halakhah*, and must be loved by his new co-religionists, never to be reminded of what he was in the past. Just as it is prohibited to oppress the orphan, so it is considered a terrible wrong to oppress a convert.

## Death, burial and mourning

This world is described in rabbinic literature as a corridor leading to the world to come. Humans have to prepare themselves in the corridor before entering the hall which is their destination. Despite this, the message of Judaism does not concentrate on death and the hereafter, but on life. Indeed, the most common greeting exchanged between Jews when drinking together is *le-haim* ('to life').

Death has its own associated rituals. Before dying, persons should confess their sins, and if possible end their life with the declaration of the first line of the *shema* on their lips: 'Hear [*shema*], O Israel, the Lord is our God, the Lord is One'. It is particularly meritorious to die affirming the oneness of God. In the presence of a dying person it is prohibited to do anything which will hasten death, active euthanasia being abhorrent to traditional Judaism.

Death is defined as the cessation of breathing, which may be tested for with a feather or a mirror. Recently some leading American Orthodox rabbis have accepted brain death, where breathing may continue on a respirator but there are no vital brain functions, as a sufficient criterion of death. This is an important innovation, though it has not won wide acceptance among halakhists, because it opens up possibilities of organ donation by Jews for transplant surgery.

A dead person should be buried as soon as possible after death, preferably on the same day. Leaving the body without burial is considered a desecration of the dead, as is cutting up the corpse in a post-mortem examination unless this is absolutely necessary. Jewish communities usually have their own *chevra kaddisha* ('holy fellowship') societies of men and women volunteers who wash the body and dress it in a shroud before placing it in a coffin. Some earth from the land of Israel is put in the coffin with the corpse so that, symbolically at least, the dead are interred in the Holy Land.

Burial takes place in consecrated ground. Orthodoxy does not permit cremation because this negates the belief in bodily resurrection in the messianic age, though many Reform rabbis will officiate at cremations. Before the funeral service begins a garment of each mourner is cut and the mourner makes the blessing: 'Blessed are you, Lord our God King of the Universe, the true Judge'. A shortened form of this blessing, *barukh dayan ha-emet*, is used by everyone whenever the death of someone is announced. Close relatives are the first to cast earth into the grave and sons recite a special version of the *kaddish* prayer at the graveside. After the funeral the family return home for a traditional mourners' feast, consisting of round foods such as hard boiled eggs and chick peas.

All members of the immediate family are in mourning for the first week after the funeral, known as *shiva* ('seven'). They stay indoors, sit on low chairs, wear a torn garment and non-leather shoes, do not shave or have a bath, and cover over all the mirrors in the house. Memorial candles are kept burning in the house of mourning for seven days and prayer services are held there. Memorial prayers for the dead are recited and members of the community come to comfort the mourners.

From the end of the *shiva* until thirty days after the death, known as *sheloshim* ('thirty'), the family are in a lesser mode of mourning. They return to normal life but avoid celebrations, particularly occasions where music is played. While spouses, parents and siblings end their mourning with the end of the *sheloshim*, children continue their semi-mourning for twelve months. Sons say the mourner's *kaddish*, a prayer praising God despite the pain of bereavement, for the first eleven months after death. The recital of *kaddish* is meant to help the soul of the deceased rise from the purgatory of *gehinnom* to heaven. If the *kaddish* were said for the full twelve months this would indicate that the deceased was a genuinely wicked person needing *kaddish* to be said for the full period.

The death anniversary, known in Yiddish as a *yahrzeit* ('year's time'), falls each year on the Hebrew date of death, and memorial prayers will be recited in synagogue on the previous *Shabbat*. The *yahrzeit* is marked by the kindling of a memorial candle, recitation of the mourners' *kaddish*, and, in some communities, by children fasting on their parents' *yahrzeits*.

## FURTHER READING

Goldin, H.E. (trans) (1963) *Code of Jewish Law*, New York, Hebrew Publishing Company.

Kaplan, A. (1983) *Made in Heaven: A Jewish Wedding Guide*, New York, Moznaim Publishing Corporation.

Lamm, M. (1969) *The Jewish Way in Death and Mourning*, New York, Jonathan David Publishers.

——— (1980) *The Jewish Way in Love and Marriage*, San Francisco, Harper & Row.

Siegel, R., Strassfeld, M. and Strassfeld, S. (1973) *The Jewish Catalog*, Philadelphia, The Jewish Publication Society of America.

Strassfeld, S. and Strassfeld, M. (1976) *The Second Jewish Catalog*, Philadelphia, The Jewish Publication Society of America.

Unterman, A. (1981) *Jews, Their Religious Beliefs and Practices*, London, Routledge & Kegan Paul.

——— (1991) *Dictionary of Jewish Lore and Legend*, London, Thames and Hudson.

Zborowski, M. and Herzog, E. (1962) *Life is With People: The Culture of the Shtetl*, New York, Schocken Books.

## Prayer Books

Orthodox: *Authorized Daily Prayer Book of the United Hebrew Congregations of the Commonwealth* (Centenary Edn), London, 1990.
Reform: *Service of the Heart: Weekday Sabbath and Festival Services and Prayers for Home and Synagogue*, London, 1967.

# 6. Sikhism

*Sewa Singh Kalsi*

Sikh rites of passage are one of the fundamental instruments of transmission and continuity of the traditional values in Sikh society. According to Uberoi, 'The obligatory and often-repeated social performance of a body of rites serves to give definitive expression and form to a people's collective life and ideas' (1988: 503). This chapter aims to demonstrate how the roles of participants in the rites of passage are closely linked to the power relationships in the Sikh social structure, i.e., rules of inheritance of property, status and the differential position of women. An analysis of the rites of ***kurmāi/ mangni*** (engagement) and *lāvān* (wedding ceremony) will be made to highlight the interrelatedness of social customs and religious beliefs. Analysis of the funeral rites provides new insight into the working of caste, religion, kinship networks and the social orientation of Sikh religious beliefs, i.e., transmigration of soul, ***mukti*** (salvation) and *awāgaun* (cycle of birth and death).

## Birth

Panjabi/Sikh society is patriarchal in authority and all inheritance is through the male line, which ensures the continuity of one's *kul* (lineage). The birth of a son ensures that one day he will perform funeral rites to save the parent's soul. Individual status is ascribed on the basis of one's birth in a particular *jāt* (caste). The term *jāt* denotes one's traditional occupation. At the village level the term *birādari* (brotherhood) is applied collectively to all the members of the same *jāt*, i.e., *Tarkhāns*' (carpenters) *birādari*; they are regarded as descendants of a common ancestor. Participation in the life-cycle rituals is obligatory for members of one's *birādari* and the *birādari panchāyat* (council) is responsible for enforcing caste *dharma* (religious and social obligations).

After the marriage the birth of a child is enthusiastically awaited by the parents. The birth of a child is regarded as *wāheygurū/rab di dāt* (gift of God). On the birth of a son there is much rejoicing and exchange of gifts, while the arrival of a daughter remains a comparatively less significant affair. The birth of a son is depicted as *puttin gandh pavey sansār* (relationship with society is established through sons) in the teachings of Sikh Gurūs (Gurū Granth Sāhib, p. 143). At the birth of a son the doors of the house are decorated with leaves from the *sirin* (Acacia sirissa) or mango tree, which are provided by the family *jheeri* (water-carrier's wife) for which she receives a ritual gift of *gurd* (raw sugar). The mother of the child remains secluded in her room for thirteen days. She is prohibited from entering the domestic kitchen because she is regarded as polluted after the birth. The period of seclusion is called *sutak* (ritual impurity).

On the thirteenth day, the mother is given a ritual bath. She discards her old clothes, which are regarded as the symbol of ritual impurity, and she wears a new set of clothes. Her discarded clothes are given to the midwife along with some food. Another important rite associated with the birth of a son is called *chhati*; usually it takes place when the boy is five weeks old. It is a big feast organised by the paternal family, to which the mother's parents, other relatives and members of one's *birādari* are invited. The mother and child receive gifts from their relatives and a small amount of money called *sagan* (auspicious gift) from *birādari* members.

The festival of *lohrdi* falls in the month of January; it is celebrated by the families in which boys have been born, by distributing *gurd*. Young men and girls in separate groups visit families of newly born boys on this day and receive a gift of *gurd*. In the evening, the family will organise a big bonfire at their home. Women of the household and their *birādari* get together and sing songs wishing long life to the newly born boy; at the end they receive a ritual gift of raw sugar. The sociological significance of the festival of *lohrdi* and the feast of *chhati* lies in the fact that they are instrumental in reinforcing and perpetuating patriarchal values among the Sikhs.

The birth of a girl is a constant reminder of her transient membership in her natal family, and that she will join her husband's household after marriage. At her wedding the father will perform the ritual of *kanayādān* (gift of a virgin to the husband) to gain the highest merit. She is also regarded as a financial liability because of the cost of her dowry and wedding. She remains a *prayee* (an outsider) in her natal family. Girls and boys are prepared for distinct roles in the family. While a girl learns to cook and sew as well as looking after young brothers and sisters, a boy is trained to take up his father's role by pursuing outdoor activities. A girl is constantly reminded of her future role of becoming a wife in someone else's house, and that her behaviour as an ideal wife will enhance the honour of her natal family.

## Naming

Traditionally children were given names by their grandparents or by *bhuā* (father's elder sister). Nowadays most Sikh families go to a gurdwara (Sikh place of worship) and ask for an initial letter of the Panjābi alphabet from the Gurū Granth Sāhib (Sikh scripture) for choosing the name for their child. The process of naming Sikh children begins with an *Ardās* (Sikh prayer) by the *granthī* (reader of the Gurū Granth Sāhib) who declares that a particular family have been blessed by a gift of a child by God, and that they seek an *akhar* (a letter) for naming their child. Afterwards the *granthī* opens the Gurū Granth Sāhib at random; and the first letter of the first word on the left hand page is announced for choosing a name for the child. The name-titles, 'Singh' and 'Kaur', were first prescribed at the *amrit* ceremony innovated by the tenth Gurū, Gobind Singh, in 1699. Nowadays, children born in Sikh families automatically get the name-title 'Singh' or 'Kaur' after their first name. Devout Sikh families ensure that a newly born baby receives *amrit* (ritually prepared nectar; it is made with water and sugar). In this case the *granthī* recites the first five verses of the Gurū Granth Sāhib while stirring the water and sugar with a short double-edged sword. He then puts some *amrit* in the baby's mouth with a miniature ceremonial sword.

## Turban

A turban is an essential part of a male Sikh's uniform. It is also worn by many Muslim and Hindu men in the sub-continent of India; a turban is regarded as a symbol of honour. There is no specific injunction concerning the age at which one should start wearing a turban. Usually a male Sikh child begins to wear a turban when he reaches the age of eleven or twelve and is able to look after it. A turban signifies the religious identity of a male Sikh. Nowadays many Sikh families organise *pagri bannān* (tying a turban) ceremony for their young sons. It is performed either at a gurdwara or at the family residence in the presence of the Gurū Granth Sāhib. After the *Ardās*, the *granthī* or an elderly Sikh person is asked to tie the turban on the boy's head. At this stage the congregation chant the Sikh slogan, *boley so nihāl – sat sri akāl* (one who says God is immortal is a happy person), signifying their approval and joy. Sikh families make a generous donation of money and food to the gurdwara on this occasion.

## Marriage

In Panjabi/Sikh society transition from childhood to adulthood is through the institution of marriage. A Panjabi girl is called *kanayā* or *kuāri* (maiden) before marriage, and a boy is called *kuāra* (bachelor). A Sikh wedding has far greater significance than the simple unification of man and woman in the matrimonial state. It is looked upon as an alliance between two families. The wedding is both a social and a religious occasion. Through the pre-wedding and wedding rituals of a Sikh marriage, insight can be gained into the complexity of kinship ties, the entanglement of religion with the social structure, and the functioning of caste and the cohesiveness of the joint family.

The concept of *sanjog* (preordained relationship) plays an important role in the establishment of a marriage alliance, which is perceived as *jithey sanjog likhyā, othey hi viāh honā* (marriage is a preordained relationship). The Sikh scriptures consider marriage to be a spiritual bond rather than a contract which unites two persons. At the beginning of the wedding ceremony the officiant utters the following words, addressed particularly to the couple, which highlight the significance of the Sikh wedding:

> The Sikh Gurūs had a very high regard for the state of marriage. They insisted that marriage is not only a civil or social contract, but that its highest and most ideal purpose is to fuse two souls into one so that they may become spiritually inseparable.
>
> (The Sikh Marriage Ceremony, Publication No. 15, The Sikh Missionary Society, Southall, UK (no date))

Guru Nanak impressed upon his followers that they should lead a worldly life, that is, the normal life of householders, recognising their duties to parents, wife and children and to the wider society. He emphatically rejected the notion of asceticism and celibacy. The high position accorded to the status of a householder by the Sikh Gurūs is demonstrated by their practical example of being married men.

At a Sikh wedding, the recital of *lāvān* (a hymn composed by the fourth Gurū, Ram Das, for his daughter's wedding) is mandatory. The four verses of *lāvān* provide the couple with advice by placing their new status within the context of union with God. The concept of *ik jot doye mūrti* (fusion of two souls into one) is strongly emphasised through various hymns recited at the wedding ceremony, e.g.:

> The bride should know no other man except her
> husband, so the Guru ordains. She alone
> is of a good family, she alone shines with light
> who is adorned with the love of her husband. There
> is only one way to the heart of the beloved, to be
> humble and true to his bidding. Only thus is true
> union attained. They are not husband and wife who
> have physical contact only. Only they are truly
> wedded who have one spirit in two bodies.
>
> (Gurū Granth Sāhib, p. 788)

The most important area in which the parents have complete control over the life of their children is in the selection of their spouses. The factors considered vital in the selection of spouses are the rules of endogamy, *got* (clan) and village exogamy. Caste endogamy is a basic criterion of marital arrangement among the Sikhs. Bhachu says, 'The aspect of the caste system that I particularly want to stress, since it relates to the subject of marriage and dowry, is that all the Sikh castes are endogamous' (1985: 180).

According to the norms of caste endogamy, 'correct' marriage partners can be found only in one's own caste group. The second rule of mate selection is that of four-*got* exogamy. The term *got* refers to a group of people within a *jāt* who claim descent from a common ancestor. In view of their common ancestry, marriage between members of the same *got* is viewed as incestuous. For example, all Rāmgarhiā Sikhs belong to the *Tarkhān* (carpenter) caste which has many *got*s, i.e., Kalsi, Sambhi, Virdee, Sond, Panesar, Matharu, Bhogal, Bahra, Sahota, Phul, etc. The principle of four-*got* exogamy states that marriage into clans of one's father, mother, father's mother and mother's mother is prohibited.

Besides caste endogamy and *got* exogamy, a third rule governing marriage is that of village exogamy. In the Panjab, a village is regarded as a single social unit or family for the purposes of mate selection. All children in the village are viewed as brothers and sisters. Thus to marry within a village is tantamount to incest. In fact, the rule of village exogamy operates as an extension of the rule of *got* exogamy. The sociological significance of the rule of village exogamy can be traced by examining the original settlement of Panjabi villages. *Mitākshrā*, the Hindu customary law of inheritance, forbids female members from inheriting ancestral property, and the rule of patrilocal residence demands that after marriage girls leave their natal village to join the husbands' families. Thus, in practice, the rule of village exogamy is also instrumental in the working of the customary law of inheritance in the Panjabi/Sikh society.

Since the institution of marriage plays an important part in maintaining boundaries between caste groups, inter-caste marriages are strongly disapproved of by the Sikhs. These marriages bring the family's *izzat* into disrepute. Reflecting on the inter-caste marriages in Southall, Bhachu says, 'There was a severe opposition to a marriage between a *Jāt* bride and a *Rāmgarhiā* groom. The bride's kin threatened to kill the groom since this was a hypogamous marriage' (1985: 75).

The process of arranging a child's marriage begins when the parents ask their relatives to look for a suitable spouse. It was a common practice to arrange marriages of fairly young children, i.e., girls between the age of thirteen and fifteen married to boys of sixteen to eighteen years old. A person who performs the role of arranging a *rishtā* (marriage) is called *bicholā*; he is responsible for providing vital information about family *gots* including particulars of would-be bride and groom, and the general status and reputation of the families concerned. Marriage negotiations are conducted in complete secrecy to avoid any embarrassment to the parties. Once the families have satisfied themselves about the *gots* and other particulars, the girl's parents ask the *bicholā* to arrange a meeting with the boy's parents to 'see' (*mundā dekhnā*) the boy. Nowadays both the girl and boy are seen by the respective families. If the parties approve the relationship, a date is fixed for the ceremony of *kurmāi/mangni* (engagement).

In Britain, the ceremony of *thākā* (reservation of a boy) is becoming very popular among the Sikhs. *Thākā* is a type of promising which precedes the engagement ceremony. Unlike the engagement ceremony, *thākā* is a quiet family affair which is performed in the presence of family members only at the boy's house. Usually the boy receives gifts of money from the girl's relatives. The engagement ceremony also takes place at the would-be groom's residence or at a local gurdwara. A party of five or seven kinsmen of the girl, usually her father, father's brothers and maternal uncles, go to perform the engagement ceremony; they carry gifts of *mathiyāi* (Indian sweets) and fruit with them. Before they enter the house, the boy's mother performs the ritual of *tel-chonā* (sprinkling mustard oil on the threshold). The ritual of *tel-chonā* symbolises the warding off of evil spirits on auspicious occasions; it has been practised by the Sikhs and Hindus over the centuries.

The engagement ceremony is performed in the presence of male relatives and members of one's *birādari*. It begins with the recital of *Ardās*. If the engagement ceremony takes place at a gurdwara, a special hymn of *kurmāi* is sung from the Gurū Granth Sāhib. Afterwards the girl's father puts seven handfuls of dried fruit in the boy's *jholi* (lap made of a pink scarf) and then he puts one *chhuārā* (dried date) in the boy's mouth. This ritual is called *sagan-denā* (giving a ritual gift), and it confirms that the alliance has been accepted by the boy's family in the presence of *birādari* members. Now the boy is called *mangiyā hoyā* (engaged); it signifies a qualitative change in his social status. At the engagement ceremony the boy receives gifts of a gold ring or bracelet and some money from the girl's father. Following the engagement ceremony, the boy's family send gifts of a long scarf and sweets for the would-be bride. This ritual is called *chuni bhejnā*. The sweets are distributed among close relatives and members of one's *birādari* as an announcement of the engagement of their daughter.

The date of the wedding is fixed by mutual consultation. Tuesdays and Thursdays are avoided as they are believed to be inauspicious days. It is customary for the girl's parents to send a *sāhey-chithi* (invitation letter) to the boy's family, inviting them for the solemnisation of marriage on an appointed day. The *sāhey-chithi* is prepared in the presence of members of one's *birādari*, and it is sprinkled with safron. This custom has a ritual significance since red is the symbol of the renewal of life (Bhattacharyya 1975: 121). In the Panjab, it used to be the customary duty of the family *nāi* (barber) to deliver *sāhey-chithi*, for which he received a ritual gift of clothes and some money. In Britain, the *sāhey-chithi* is delivered by the matchmaker.

The invitation letter sent out to relatives and friends in Britain is printed in English and Panjābi. It bears miniature imprints of the Sikh emblem at the top. The first part of the invitation letter is devoted to the invocation of God by printing a couplet in Panjābi, which reads:

*satgur dātey kāj rachāyā, apni mehr karāyi*
*dātā kāraj āp sawārey, ih usdi wadyāi*

(Great God ordained this auspicious occasion, and he will see it successfully concluded – in it lies his greatness).

Two days before the wedding, the ritual of *māyian* is performed at their respective homes. The prospective bride or groom is seated on a wooden plank called *patri*, and a red cloth is held above by four female relatives, while married women of the *birādari*, led by the mother, rub paste of turmeric, flour and mustard oil on his or her face, arms and legs. During this ritual they sing traditional songs. At the culmination of *māyian*, women receive a ritual gift of *gogley* (Panjabi sweets especially cooked for weddings).

On the day before the wedding, the ritual of *sānt-krauni* is performed, when the bride's maternal uncle makes a gift of clothes and some jewellery called *nānkey-shak*, including *churā* (a row of red ivory bangles). He puts the bangles on his niece while the women sing traditional songs depicting the role of a maternal uncle. After the ritual bath, the bride wears clothes provided by her maternal uncle for the wedding ceremony. The bridegroom also receives from his maternal uncle *jorā-jāmā* (a set of clothes) which he wears at the wedding ceremony. Ritual gifts of *nānkey-shak* and *jorā-jāmā* signify the importance of the role of the mother's natal family at the pre-wedding and wedding rituals. Her children get married wearing clothes provided by her parents, which reinforces the alliance established at her own wedding, and her brother plays the second most important role at the wedding rituals next to her husband.

## *BARĀT* (WEDDING PARTY)

All male relatives and male members of the boy's *birādari* comprise the wedding party. The ceremony of *vāg-pharāyi/injerdi* (groom's sisters and female cousins hold on to his pink scarf, symbolising the bridle of a horse) takes place when the wedding party leaves for the bride's village. The bridegroom makes gifts of money to his female relatives, who sing traditional songs wishing him a safe return with his wife. The ritual of *vāg-pharāyi* symbolises the traditional image of the groom as that of a knight riding at the head of armed men who go to claim his beloved. It is interesting to note that the marriage ceremony is called *vivāh* in Panjābi, derived from the root, *vāhā*, meaning to carry.

The wedding party is received by the kinsmen of the bride at a *janjgarh* (hall reserved for wedding parties) or a gurdwara where the ceremony of *milni* (ritual meeting of the heads of both families) takes place in the presence of *birādari* members. The ceremony begins with *Ardās* recited by the *granthī*, who prays for God's blessing on the alliance of the bride's and the groom's families. Then the first *milni* of the *kurmān* (bride's father and groom's father) takes place when the bride's father makes a ritual gift of a turban and some money to the groom's father. It is followed by the *milni* of *māmein* (maternal uncles of the bride and groom). The bride's maternal uncle makes a ritual gift of one turban and some money to the groom's maternal uncle. Usually a list of important relatives is prepared by the groom's family, and they receive a ritual gift of a turban and some money from the bride's father. The ritual of *milni* is restricted to those kinsmen who are related to the father through blood or marriage, i.e., grandfather, father's brother, sister's husband and sons-in-law. Friends of the groom's family do not receive any gifts, which signifies the nature of the ritual of *milni* as a marker of boundaries between kin and other relationships.

## *ĀNAND KĀRAJ* (WEDDING CEREMONY)

After the ritual of *milni*, the wedding party is ready to enter the reception hall for breakfast. Before they go in, the bride's mother performs the ritual of *tel-chonā* and *kumbh* (a jug full of water in which the groom's father puts some coins is held by one of the bride's female relatives). In the Panjab, a family *jheeri* (water-carrier's wife) carries the jug, and she receives the money poured into the jug as her ritual gift. The ritual of *kumbh* symbolises the worship of the Hindu water-god, Khāwājā. After the breakfast, the wedding party moves into the congregation hall for the wedding ceremony.

The main pattern of Sikh marriage in Britain is *ānand kāraj*, coupled with the legal requirement of registering the marriage. At the wedding ceremony, the presence of the Gurū Granth Sāhib is mandatory. First the groom sits in front of the Gurū Granth Sāhib, followed by the bride, who sits on his left. The wedding ceremony begins with *Ardās*, seeking God's *āgiyā* (permission), followed by the ritual of *pallā-pharānā* (joining the couple with the scarf worn by the groom) performed by the bride's father. The ritual of *pallā-pharānā* is very emotional, when a father gives away his daughter as a *kanyādān* (gift of a virgin). Gupta says, 'Giving a *kanayā*'s hand or *dān* (ritual gift) is considered among the holiest acts in the life of a parent' (1974: 91). In the absence of her father, either her elder brother or paternal uncle performs the ritual of *pallā-pharānā*. At this stage the *rāgīs* (religious musicians) sing the hymn of *palley taindey lāgi* from the Gurū Granth Sāhib, which stresses the permanence of the marital bond. The main message of this hymn is the pledge by the bride:

> Praise and blame I forsake both. I hold the edge of your garment/scarf. All else I let pass. All relationships I have found false. I cling to thee my lord.
>
> (Gurū Granth Sāhib, p. 963)

Now the reading and singing of four verses of *lāvān* (wedding hymn) begins. After the reading of each verse the couple walks round the Gurū Granth Sāhib in a clockwise direction, the bridegroom leading the bride. The circumambulation is repeated four times. The ceremony concludes with the recital of the hymn of *ānand sāhib* from the Gurū Granth Sāhib, and *Ardās*. The couple remain seated in front of the Gurū Granth Sāhib until the ritual of *sagan* (ritual gift) is performed by the bride's mother. She brings a *thāl* (plate made of steel) full of *ladoo*s (Indian sweets) and a coconut, which is a symbol of fertility. First she puts the coconut in the bridegroom's *jholi* and then she puts a *ladoo* in the mouth of the bridegroom and bride; afterwards she puts all the *ladoo*s and some money in the bridegroom's *jholi*. At this stage the groom's father performs the ritual of *bori-vārnā*. He carries a bag made of red material, which is full of coins. He passes the bag over the heads of his son and daughter-in-law a couple of times, enjoying the newly acquired status of father-in-law. Traditionally, the coins are thrown over the couple by the groom's father at the time of *doli* (bride leaving her natal home with her husband). The ritual of *bori-vārnā* signifies the public demonstration of the father-in-law gaining a daughter-in-law.

### *DOLI TORNĀ*

*Doli* is a kind of sedan in which the bride is carried to her husband's home by four *jheer* (water-carrier) men. The ceremony of *doli-tornā* takes place after lunch when the groom, accompanied by his father and some kinsmen, go to the bride's house. They receive all the items of dowry. Before the bride leaves her natal home she changes into clothes provided by her husband's family. The bridegroom leads the bride out of her natal home while she holds on to his *pallā* (pink scarf). Her female relatives sing traditional songs depicting the separation of a daughter from her parents. The ritual of *doli-tornā* symbolises the permanent change in the bride's status from being a member of her father's descent group to being a member of her husband's; it is expressed in terms of moving from being a *dhee* (daughter) to being a *noonh* (daughter-in-law).

Now the wedding party returns to their native town, where they are received by the groom's mother and other female relatives for the performance of the ritual of *pani-vārnā*. The bride and the bridegroom are made to wait outside the main door. The groom's mother carries a jug full of *kachi-lassi* (mixture of milk and water) which she passes over the heads of her son and daughter-in-law seven times, taking a sip each time. At the end, she performs the ritual of *sagan-denā* by putting a *ladoo* in the mouth of her son and daughter-in-law. She now performs the ritual of *tel-chonā*, and allows the couple to enter the house followed by members of the wedding party. It is a big moment in a woman's life when she becomes the mother of a married son in the village, a mother-in-law (*sas* in Panjābi) in her own right.

The bride spends only one night at her husband's house and returns to her natal home the following day accompanied by her husband. A son-in-law is called *prauhnā* (guest) with affection by his wife's relatives, while the term *juāyi* is applied in a formal discourse. The most important post-wedding ritual is called *muklāwā* (permanent change of residence and consummation of marriage). In the Panjab, there used to be a gap of a few years between the wedding and *muklāwā*, depending on the age of the bride. In Britain, it usually takes place one day after the wedding. The bride receives more gifts from her parents for the members of her husband's family. There is the now-permanent departure of the daughter from her natal home. After a few days the ritual of *got-kanālā* is performed at the groom's house. Newly married women of the *birādari* are invited for a meal to eat with the new bride; they all sit around a large dish full of food and communally eat from it. The ritual of sharing food signifies the symbolic incorporation of the bride into her husband's *got* (clan).

## Death

The incidence of death is perceived as an ultimate reality by the Sikhs. A number of phrases are applied to describe the death of a person, i.e., *purā ho giyā* (completed his span of life), *surgwās ho giyā* (has taken abode in heaven), *sansār yātrā poori kar giyā* (has completed pilgrimage of this world) and *rab dā bhānā* (divine will).

At the time of death, the first step is the performance of the ritual of *dharti te paunā* (lifting of the body from the bed on to the ground). The doors are kept open so that the *ātmā/rooh* is not trapped inside the house. The ritual of *dharti te paunā* consists of two components, religious and social. The religious part is linked with the belief in *dharti-matā* (mother-earth). Reflecting on the significance of the mother-earth, Guru Nanak wrote: '*pavan gurū pāni pitā, mātā dharat mahat*' (Air is the *gurū*; Water the father and Earth the great mother) (Gurū Granth Sāhib, p. 8). The social aspect of this ritual deals with the concept of *dekh-bhāl* (care of the deceased). Death on a bed is talked about in the *birādari* as a symbol of neglect of the deceased person. The *birādari* members would say, 'Look, there was nobody with him at the last moment; the poor man died on the bed'. Dying on the bed is not only a social stigma but it is also regarded as *bud-sagni* (most inauspicious occurrence). In this case the performance of a second *gati* (ritual for the release of soul) at the town of Peoha is prescribed. The bed is either burnt or given to the *chuhri* (sweeper's wife).

The term 'funeral' is too narrow for comprehending the meanings of pre- and post-funeral rites. There are series of ceremonies which are an integral part of the ritual of a funeral, called *antam-sanskār* (last rite) in Panjābi. The ceremony of lighting the pyre is called *agni-bhaint* (Agni is the Hindu god of fire and *bhaint* means ritual offering); it symbolises the making of an offering of one's body to the god of fire. Thus, death is not conceived of as the end of life, but is seen as a gradual transition from earthly existence to existence in heaven.

First, the body is given a ritual bath before it is dressed in new clothes and made ready to be placed on a bier. The washing of the body is called *antam-ishnān* (last bath); it is symbolic of ritual purification of the body before it is presented as an offering to the god of fire. There seems to be a structural relationship between *antam-ishnān*, *agni-bhaint* and offerings made to God at a gurdwara or a temple. Although the dead body is regarded as highly polluted, the ceremony of *antam-ishnān* is perceived as transforming the deceased person from being polluted to being ritually pure. At the death of a *suhāgaṇ* (married woman), her shroud is provided by her natal family and she is dressed as a bride; it is the symbol of the fulfilment of her wish to die before her husband.

### *MODHĀ-DENĀ* (PARTICIPATION IN CARRYING THE BIER)

The bier is carried by the sons and brothers of the deceased, led by the chief mourner, the eldest son. Only male agnates of the deceased are eligible to take part in this ritual. Women are forbidden to participate in the carrying of the bier. The rite of *modhā-denā* is structurally linked to the rules of inheritance. According to the rules of *Mitākshrā* (Hindu law of inheritance) only the *spindā*s (male descendants) are eligible to inherit ancestral property.

### *DHAMĀLAK-BHANANĀ* (BREAKING OF THE EARTHEN POT)

When the funeral procession arrives near the cremation ground the bier is lowered on to the ground. Starting from the head, the chief mourner makes an unbroken circle around the bier with water pouring from an earthen pot. As soon as he reaches the starting point he throws the pot on the ground with force so that it breaks into several pieces; this is regarded as a symbol of the release of the soul. Afterwards the bier is carried to the cremation ground for the ritual of *agni-bhaint*. Although Sikh women accompany the funeral procession, they do not go beyond this point and are forbidden to enter the cremation ground. Before the performance of the ritual of *agni-bhaint*, the *granthī* recites the *Ardās* invoking God's *āgiyā* to perform the ceremony, and also for the abode of the departed soul in God's house (*mirtak di rooh noon apney charnān wich niwās bakhshin*).

In India, ashes are collected after three days and they are deposited in the river Ganges at Hardwar with the assistance of a family Brahman. He receives a ritual gift of clothes, utensils and some money for performing the ritual of *gati* (release of soul). Writing in the early twentieth century, Macauliffe observed:

> Notwithstanding the Sikh Gurūs' powerful denunciation of Brahmans, secular Sikhs now rarely do anything without their assistance. Brahmans

help them to be born, help them to die, and help their souls after death to obtain a state of bliss.

(Macauliffe 1909: vii)

## CUSTOM OF *PAGRI* (RITUAL TRANSFER OF PATERNAL AUTHORITY)

The ritual of *pagri* (literally a turban), an ancient Indian custom, takes place after the funeral. It is an integral part of the ritual feast called *akath* (gathering of relatives and members of one's *birādari*). It is through the performance of the rite of *pagri* that the son inherits his father's status and becomes the head of the household. The ceremony begins after the culmination of *bhog* (reading of the Gurū Granth Sāhib), organised by the deceased's family for the peace of the departed soul. The chief mourner sits in front of the Gurū Granth Sāhib and receives a turban from his maternal uncle. He wears this turban in the presence of relatives and members of his *birādari*, discarding the old one. Thereafter, he is reminded of his new status and responsibilities by the senior members of his *birādari*. Now he joins the elders of the *birādari* for a communal meal, having been ritually accepted as the head of his household.

The social function of the rite of *pagri* is to facilitate the gradual incorporation of the son into the role of his father. It is argued that the role of the chief mourner in the funeral rites is implicitly linked to his eligibility to inherit his father's status as well as the ancestral property. Dermot Killingley says, 'In Hindu society, and indeed in South Asian society as a whole, one of the factors differentiating ritual procedures is the status inherited by the principal or principals from their parents' (1991: 2). Women's exclusion from the main funeral rites, i.e., *modhā-denā*, *dhamālak-bhananā* and *agni-bhaint* is a clear indication of their differential status.

## *BURĀ PAUNĀ*

In Panjābi, a widow is called *vidwā* or *randi* (*randi* literally means a prostitute – it is also used as a swear word). The status of widowhood condemns a Sikh woman to the state of perpetual *sutak* (ritual pollution). Her participation in wedding rituals is regarded as inauspicious. After the death of her husband she remains secluded for thirteen days. She discards her colourful clothes and wears a white *chuni* (long scarf), which signifies her state of mourning. The ritual of *burā-paunā* is performed on the thirteenth day after the death of her husband. She is given a ritual bath; her old clothes are discarded and she wears a new set of clothes provided by her natal family. The most significant change in her dress is the coloured scarf. Now she discards her white scarf, which is a symbol of *sutak*.

The Sikhs practise widow remarriage, which takes the form of *karevā/chādar-paunā*. In this ceremony the groom marries a widow by placing a bed sheet over her head in the presence of relatives and members of the *birādari*. A widow is not entitled to the religious wedding (*ānand-kāraj*) because she cannot be given as a *kanyādān* (ritual gift of a virgin).

## *Amrit* (Sikh initiation)

The Sikh initiation ceremony, called *amrit*, is part of the founding of the *Khālsā* (Sikh order, brotherhood, instituted by the tenth Gurū, Gobind Singh, in 1699). At that time all Sikhs had Hindu names and there was no prescribed code of discipline concerning membership of the Sikh tradition. The *Khālsā* code of discipline prescribed the wearing of Five Ks (unshorn hair, comb, steel bracelet, pair of breeches and sword). The first five neophytes (*panj piārey*), after the initiation, discarded their Hindu names and acquired the name-title 'Singh'. They drank *amrit* (nectar) from the same bowl and took three vows, individually proclaiming: 'my father is Guru Gobind Singh', 'my mother is Sahib Kaur' and 'my place of birth is Anand Pur'. The innovation of *amrit* was a fundamental statement of group identity, and it was greatly instrumental in creating a separate and distinctive Sikh community. As Uberoi says, 'Every initiation rite evidently possesses the nature of an investiture or conferment, since through it some new status with its consequent rights and obligations is conferred symbolically upon the neophyte, and he or she enters on a new mode of existence' (1975: 505).

In the late nineteenth century, the Singh Sabha (Sikh reform movement) élite achieved remarkable success in generating the process of restructuring new Sikh identity by modifying their traditional rites of passage. For example, as a result of their determined campaign, eventually in 1901, the *Ānand* (Sikh) Marriage

Act was passed by the British government. It was a unique moment in the history of struggle for a separate and a distinctive identity. Commenting on the significance of the role of powerful social groups, Geertz writes:

> Ideas – religious, moral, practical, aesthetic – must be carried by powerful social groups; someone must revere them, celebrate them, defend them, impose them. They have to be institutionalised in order to find not just an intellectual existence in society, but, so to speak, a material one as well.
>
> (Geertz 1973: 314)

In 1945, the Shiromani Gurdwara Parbandhak Committee (supreme religious body of the Sikhs constituted under the Sikh Gurdwara Act, 1925) approved the *Rahit Maryādā* (a guide to the Sikh way of life) (Cole and Sambhi 1978: 168). The *Rahit Maryādā* is a radical innovation concerning the social and religious practices of the Sikhs. The impact of codified funeral rituals was minimal on the centuries-old practices which the Sikhs share with the Hindus.

## Situation in the Sikh diaspora

There are some distinct changes in the funeral rites among the Sikh communities abroad. For example, in East Africa and the United Kingdom the Sikhs discarded the custom of lowering the dead body on to the ground. In East Africa the dead body was carried on an open bier, whereas in the United Kingdom the Sikhs have accepted the use of a coffin. Commenting on the first funeral of a Sikh migrant in Leeds, one Sikh informant said:

> The sight of the *dabbā* (coffin) shocked everyone of us. We never used coffins in East Africa and India. It is against our tradition. When you put the body in a coffin, the *ātmā* (soul) gets trapped inside the coffin. In India, when a person died all the doors of the house were kept open until the funeral. The body was always carried on an open bier so that the soul of the deceased leaves the body freely. We had never heard about the firms of funeral directors; it seems to be a good business. But how one could make money by disposing of the dead; it is beyond my comprehension.

## Conclusion

I have shown that the Sikh rites of passage are one of the fundamental instruments of transmission and continuity of traditional cultural values. Although the form of some rituals has changed outwardly, the content still remains traditional. Now, the chanting of brahmanical hymns has been replaced by readings from the Gurū Granth Sāhib, and the role of traditional intermediaries like Brahmans has been taken over by the Sikh *granthīs*. Analysis of the rituals of *akath* and *pagri* clearly demonstrates the patriarchal nature of Sikh society and dominance of the institution of *birādari* in everyday social intercourse. The Sikhs have reluctantly accepted the use of a coffin instead of taking the dead in an open bier. At the crematorium, the chief mourner does not light the pyre but instead pushes the coffin into the furnace, which is symbolic of the ritual of *lāmbu-launā* (lighting the pyre).

### FURTHER READING


Bhachu, P. (1985) *Twice-Migrants: East African Sikh Settlers in Britain*, London, Tavistock.

Bhattacharyya, N.N. (1975) *Ancient Indian Rituals and Their Social Context*, London, Curzon Press.

Cole, O. and Sambhi, P. (1978) *The Sikhs: Their Religious Beliefs and Practices*, London, Routledge & Kegan Paul.

Gupta, G.R. (1974) *Marriage, Religion and Society*, London, Curzon Press.

Geertz, C. (1973) *The Interpretation of Cultures*, New York, Basic Books.

Hershman, P. (1981) *Punjabi Kinship and Marriage*, Delhi, Hindustan Publishing Corporation.

Jyoti, S.K. (1983) *Marriage Practices of the Sikhs*, New Delhi, Deep and Deep Publications.

Kalsi, S.S. (1992) *The Evolution of a Sikh Community in Britain: Religious and Social Change among the Sikhs in Leeds and Bradford*, Leeds, Department of Theology and Religious Studies, University of Leeds.

Killingley, D. (1991) 'Introduction', in S.Y. Killingley (ed.) *Hindu Ritual and Society*, Newcastle upon Tyne, Grevatt and Grevatt.

Macauliffe, M.A. (1909) *The Sikh Religion*, Oxford, Clarendon Press.

McLeod, W.H. (1989) *Who is a Sikh?: The Problem of Sikh Identity*, Oxford, Clarendon Press.

McMullen, C.O. (1989) *Religious Beliefs and Practices of the Sikhs in Rural Punjab*, Delhi, Manohar Publications.
Oberoi, H.S. (1988) 'From Ritual to Counter Ritual', in J.T. O'Connell, M. Israel and W.G. Oxtoby (eds) *The Sikh History and Religion in the Twentieth Century*, Toronto, University of Toronto.
Singh, Kahan (1973) *Ham Hindu Nahin*, Amritsar, Sri Guru Singh Sabha Shatabdi (first Panjābi edition, 1898).
Uberoi, J.P.S. (1975) 'The Five Symbols of Sikhism', in Harbans Singh (ed.) *Perspectives on Gurū Nānak*, Patiala, Punjabi University.

# 7. Chinese Religions

*Xinzhong Yao*

Ceremonies or rites are essential parts of Chinese culture. In these ceremonies, three evolutionary components are prominent: primitive rites, syncretic ceremonies and popular rituals. Primitive rites arose along with Chinese civilisation, and played an important role in the early development of Chinese political and religious life. After that, although these rites continued to exert their influence, their prominence gradually gave way to new ceremonies which took shape in a syncretic stream of philosophy, religion and politics. Lastly, popular rituals, which were formed by a combination of popular beliefs, religious ceremonies and local customs, were and still are practised in family, village, or other communities. When these rites, ceremonies and rituals are aimed at leading a person to pass through various phases of human life, they are what will be discussed in this chapter – 'rites of passage'. The traditional Chinese take the stages as human reflections of the rhythm of cosmic movement and endow them with so much value that the corresponding ceremonies are believed to be the foundation not only of personal happiness but also of social harmony. Therefore, appropriate ceremonies for these stages must be practised to reveal their underlying meaning and to help individuals pass them smoothly.

The rites of passage in Chinese society have been under the influence of three institutional religions. The first is Confucianism. Although Confucianism is not a religion in some senses of this term, its emphasis on rites, rituals and ceremonies is not less than that of other religions. The role of Confucianism in 'rites of passage' is twofold. One is its supervision of social life and emphasis that everything must be done according to *li* (proprieties, rites or ceremonies); without *li*, life activities would become the instinct of beasts. The other is its tendency to secularity, which is responsible for the transformation of 'rites of passage' from pure religious practices to customs and family observances. For Taoism, there is a difference between philosophical Taoism and religious Taoism in regard to rites of passage. The former called for following the nature of *tao*, so it generally did not stress any rites or ceremonies which were regarded as human-made and as against nature. But later when Taoist religion emerged, this kind of Taoist philosophy was used as the basis of, and was developed into, a cult of immortality; the importance of the rites of passage increased and special ceremonies in some stages of life became necessary for those people who wanted to attain *tao*. In this new frame, Taoist rites of passage were practised and understood in the light of the theories of *yin-yang* and Five Elements, which then became dominant in popular beliefs and practices. The third religion is Buddhism. Buddhists were concerned with life after death. Their interests in the rites of passage concentrated on how to explain the relation between this life and the life to be. From this came the special ceremonies for the funeral, which were again combined with other observances and local customs, and became one of the most significant 'rites' in Chinese religion.

When we examine the roles of these three religions in the rites of passage, we find that Confucianism had a strong hold in the upper class, especially in the literati families, with more emphasis being placed on the moral significance of the rites than on their religious mysticism, while Taoism and Buddhism exerted great influence on the lower classes; the first consideration of the common people was always the relationship between the secular world and the spiritual world. However, in the past several hundred years, not only has the line between Taoist rites and Buddhist rites been obscured so much that it is almost impossible to distinguish them, but also the distance between the Confucian family and the ordinary family has been reduced and their differences in attitudes towards the rites of passage are of importance only as a curiosity. Their theories and practices are based on a common understanding that 'rites of passage' are essential for human beings to be in harmony with heaven and earth, and can function as a path from the temporary and secular to the eternal and sacred.

The rites of passage in China are rich and varied, but four are of prominence, i.e., the rites of birth, adulthood, marriage, and death: in all of these we find a strong belief that they form necessary links in the life of the whole family. The meaning of these phases can be found only in the family context and in the cycle from life to death and from death to life. What will be discussed below is mainly concerned with the traditional ways, though most of these ways are still practised in the mainland of China (perhaps with less religious meaning) and in Chinese communities all over the world.

## Birth

The traditional Chinese hold a dual attitude towards birth. On the one hand, birth means a new descendant of the family, which should be as large as possible. On the other, birth is considered inauspicious since it is accompanied by the ritually polluting blood. On account of these two considerations, varied rites are practised.

A combination of the essence of heaven and of the earth is believed to be the beginning of life, and a harmonious relation between human beings and the cosmos is necessary for a healthy pregnancy. To maintain or not to disturb this harmony, one should faithfully perform one's duties. Therefore, a due pregnancy comes only as a reward to the family for the meritorious parents or ancestors. The position of a pregnant woman in the traditional family depended on her original position. Generally speaking, the first pregnancy of the wife of the first son was taken care of more carefully, both because she was probably carrying the heir-to-be of the whole family and because this was the most dramatic event the newly wed couple had ever experienced. Besides the social care from the family members, the protection and blessing of the spiritual powers was also needed. Therefore pregnant women were expected to pray to the guardian and protective gods in the home, especially those who were in charge of the foetus and the childbirth. She or her female representatives also should visit the temples and look for the mercy of one or more deities, usually the Buddhist goddess Kuan Yin. In this aspect, rites were composed of such religious acts as piously burning incense to gods or goddesses, making vows to them, offering sacrifices to them, or simply praying for their help and protection. These acts were not only for the blessing of the child, but also for a smooth childbirth for the devotee herself. The vows varied from place to place, but usually were composed of such conditional wishes as, 'I will visit the temple or burn incense before the god every day if . . .'; 'I will repair the temple or remould a golden statue of the god if . . .'; 'I will give such and such money to the temple if . . .'.

Concerning the process of birth, there are many rituals, taboos and practices. The religious taboos were set up in the belief that birth was always accompanied by inauspicious blood. In a traditional family, a woman who had given, or would give, birth to a child was usually confined within a limited space, such as her room, where only her husband or female relatives were allowed to enter. In order to counteract its inauspiciousness, red colour, which was believed to be an auspicious colour, was used to decorate the room and door curtains. For a whole month the new mother would stay within this room; the windows of the room should not be open and the new mother was not allowed to move around. In the religious sense, these taboos or rituals were to avoid offending the family gods who disliked the birth blood. In the practical sense, they were designed to protect the new mother from diseases and help her recover quickly. The new mother, bleeding so much at giving birth, was believed to be so weak and vulnerable that the evil forces, especially wind and cold water, would bring irrecoverable damage to her health.

When a new descendant came along, various celebrations were held, although their extent was different in the case of the first boy from that in the case of other boys or girls. The ceremony for a boy normally was more significant than that for a girl. The *Book of Rites* records that a bow should be placed on the left of the door if the child was a boy and a handkerchief on the right of the door if a girl (Legge 1968: Vol. XXVII 471). Since the left was thought to be nobler and more valuable than the right, and the bow was more useful than the handkerchief, the difference between these two kinds of ceremonies was quite obvious. The celebrations usually took place on the third day, on the thirtieth day, on the hundredth day and on the first birthday, and consisted of many special rites, such as the 'rites of shaving', the 'rites of meeting the child's maternal uncle', the 'rites of giving the child a little name' and so forth. The more important rites were carried on at two levels. As religious rituals, they included offerings being made to ancestors, to family gods and to other deities, partly for expressing gratitude for their blessing and protection and partly for reporting the arrival of the new member. As social ceremonies, colleagues, friends and relatives, especially those from the side of the new mother, were invited. The guests would bring the baby such gifts as red eggs, babies' garments, and other rare things, such as silver locks which were believed to lock the soul within the body so that the child would enjoy a long life.

## Adulthood

Having been born in a family, a child begins his or her long journey of life. While growing up, the child was educated and trained in the family rules and duties and tradition, varying from family to family. Most Confucian families preferred to follow the description of these training programmes recorded in *Li Chi*, or the *Book of Rites*, a collection of rituals or ceremonies of ancient China. For example, when boys were seven, they were taught not to sit closely with girls; at eight, they learnt the etiquette of entering and leaving, eating and drinking – for example, how to greet the grandparents, parents or elders when coming back home or how to say goodbye to them when leaving, how to show their gratitude to the ancestors before any eating or drinking; at ten, they learnt the different classes of characters and calculation, and the behaviour of a youth and the ways of polite conversation; at thirteen, they began to learn music, recite poetry, and practise the dance of the ancient time. These teachings and practices prepared them for their adulthood which arrived when they reached a certain age.

The age when a child is regarded as an adult varies from place to place and from time to time. Some stipulate that the sixteenth birthday be the symbol of maturity; others insist that a child should not be called a grown-up until he or she is eighteen, while the *Book of Rites* records that a child reaches adulthood at twenty. This is signified by the performance of the 'rites of capping' for a boy and the rites of hairdo or coiffure for a girl. The ritual of this kind is an initiation ceremony for children to attain adulthood and to enter social life. It is true that, even in the past, the rites of adulthood were practised only in a limited number of Chinese families; however, since these families were the centre of political and social life, and their influence was far-reaching and they were imitated by other families, we should not dismiss their significance, as some western scholars tend to do. Of the rites for the boy and the rites for the girl, the former are more widely performed. According to the description of the *Book of Rites*, the rites of capping include three steps: preparation, capping and after capping.

Traditionally, boys could not have any cap on and could not take part in the formal ceremonies until they reached a certain age and performed the rites of capping. For this ritual, a proper and sacred time had to be found by divining with the *I Ching*, a ceremony held in the ancestral temple, under the supervision of the boy's father. If the date suggested by the father was auspicious, the divination ceremony would come to an end; otherwise, another date had to be re-divined on the next day, until an auspicious date was obtained. It was very important for the ceremony to be approved by divination, which was thought of as a validation of the spiritual world. After the time was fixed, the father had to decide, again in the light of the divination, who should be invited and to whom he should send formal invitations. Among these guests, the most honourable was invited as the principal guest who would help the father to conduct the whole ceremony.

By now everything was ready, and the ceremony of capping was due to take place. On the day, the guests, in formal clothes, came and were met by the father and the boy. They bowed to each other. In due course, the principal guest, or the master of ceremonies, capped the boy three times, representing the blessing from heaven, earth and the water underworld, or simply each adding more honour and lending more importance to his coming of age (Legge 1968: Vol. XXVIII 426). For each capping, the boy had to put on suitable clothes and comb his hair carefully, while the guests had to wash their hands and perform specific rituals. In due course, the father – the master of ceremonies – would announce, usually in such a formula: 'in this auspicious month and on this lucky day, we endue you with the cap for the first time. Put away your childish thoughts from now on, and see that you keep guard upon the virtues of your manhood. Then shall your years all be fair, and your good fortune grow from more to more.'

Having been capped, the boy had now become a man with his new name, which was his 'great name', symbolising his maturity and differentiating him from his childhood; from then, he should not be treated as a boy any longer. The special rites were designed to stress his new status. He first visited his mother, and they bowed to each other. Then he visited his brothers and cousins, receiving their congratulations and exchanging bows with each one. He then visited and greeted his other relatives, both male and female. He also had to ask permission to visit, and on a suitable occasion, went to see, his superiors or other officials and his father's colleagues, presenting them with gifts, since now he was ready to carry all the duties of a man and of a subject.

Capping in the Chinese context is not simply a ceremony through which young people are admitted into adulthood and maturity; more significance of this rite is to be found in the structure of the family. The performance of the whole rite is under the supervision of the father, the master of ceremonies. The divining and capping took place in the ancestral temple, which aimed not only at informing their ancestors, but also at showing that the son would in due time take his place in this life-cycle of the family. By capping, a boy became a full-grown man with all the duties of a son, a brother, a subject, and a legal citizen, i.e., with filial and fraternal duties, loyal service and deferential submission.

## Marriage

The next step for an adult is marriage, which is so important for the family that its rites are always regarded as the most prominent of the rites of passage in Chinese society. Marriage is, like birth, a link in the chain of the lineage. Therefore, it is not only an event between two young persons, but a bond between two surnames – two families. One of its functions is to secure the continuance of the lineage and to enlarge the family tree.

The belief in marriage as predestined was very popular with ordinary people. It was believed that there was a marriage god, the Old Man under the Moon or the Old Man of the Moon. This god arranged all the marriages of the people on earth according to their fate and used red cords to tie the couple-to-be together. However, the Chinese also believed that the fate of a marriage could be changed through continuing effort and correct moral and religious behaviour; this could move the gods and enable the person concerned to obtain permission for a marriage or change the fate of the marriage. In the social context, the belief in the god of marriage was replaced by the necessity of the go-between for any arrangement of marriage.

Marriage is the very act to establish a new family or a nuclear unit of the clan. Therefore, to arrange a good marriage for a young boy or girl is the first concern of the parents. In the traditional way, this arrangement must be initiated by a mediator – a matchmaker, usually a professional or amateur woman, or a relative or friend of both families. First, the go-between had to carry the proposal from the boy's family to the girl's family and ask for the year, month, day and hour of the girl's birth, which are called 'eight characters' because they are presented by eight Chinese characters in four pairs, each pair consisting of one of the Heavenly Stems and one of the Earthly Branches. If the go-between was given the girl's 'eight characters', this was regarded as a sign of preliminary consent. Then the boy's family or both families respectively sent their 'eight characters' to the diviners and found out whether or not the boy and the girl were suitable for each other. The time of birth was essential for the consideration of marriage between them, because it was viewed as connected with certain supernatural forces that would affect not only their own future life but also the future life of the whole family, and result in the prosperousness or decline of the next generation. Therefore, whom one should marry and whether a marriage would be a happy one were mainly decided by the balance of two spiritual forces present at the time of their birth. For example, a 'tiger' girl could not marry a 'chicken' boy, the former being too overwhelming a power for the latter and even for the latter's parents. When the result of divination was auspicious, the two families began to make contact, sometimes still through the matchmaker, to find a date for the betrothal, which was also to be validated by the divining.

Comparatively speaking, the betrothal was less complicated than the first step. Usually, on the arranged day, the boy's mother or father, accompanied by the matchmaker and/or other relatives, went to the girl's family and handed over presents and money to the girl's family as the gifts of engagement. If the arrangement was agreed, a sort of banquet was provided by the girl's family for them; at the same time, the boy's family also held some kind of celebration, which marked the betrothal. After that, the betrothal gifts, such as clothing, silver ornaments or jewellery and money, should be sent by the boy's family to the girl and her family, and the dowry was sent by the girl's family to the boy's home several days before the wedding. There were very strict restrictions on the nature and number of the gifts. The gifts should be auspicious and their amount should be an even number.

The wedding day at last came; the girl was going to leave her own family to enter another family, and the boy's family would receive a 'new member'. Before leaving her home, the bride performed ceremonial prostrations to the ancestral tablets, to the parents and grandparents if any, and to the family gods, thanking them for their care. Then she was sent by her relatives, riding in a sedan chair or some other kind of vehicle, from her original home to the home-to-be, and was greeted by the bridegroom and his relatives. Starting from the moment of leaving, she was expected to express her sorrow in a suitable way, showing her reluctance to leave her family, but should stop when she arrived at her destination. She entered the house covered with a red cloth, and led in by the bridegroom. With the offerings of food, fruit and flowers, the couple first paid homage to Heaven and Earth, to ancestors, and to the family gods, burning incense and bowing, in order to get spiritual validation of the marriage. Then they bowed to each other three times, showing their agreement to this marriage. They also had to bow to their parents, uncles, aunts, elder brothers and sisters, and any senior relatives present, in order to get the social validation of the marriage. After this, the feast of the marriage began which usually lasted until midnight or even later, though the new couple had retreated to their 'new' room.

## Death

When talking about burial customs in China, Burkhardt points out, 'In a land where such reverence is displayed to the departed it is only natural to announce that the rite connected with the dead is of primary importance' (Burkhardt 1953: 176). From the viewpoint of the rites of passage, death is the last phase, which signals the completion of a life-cycle. Technically, the rites for death have three parts: the efforts of recovering the 'deceased'; the mourning; and the funeral.

Death was believed to be caused by the departing of the soul from its body. In the hope that this departure was only temporary, as in the case of a dream, some actions were performed to avoid taking a false death as a real one. When a senior member died, such practices were required immediately to check if it was final or not. Somebody, usually the dead person's intimate, went to the roof from the front side of the house in which the dead person used to live, facing north, which was believed to be the area of the *yin* world, carrying the dead person's clothes, and shouting three times, 'So and so, return!' Then he or she quickly descended from the back side of the house and carried the clothes, which were believed to be possibly carrying the wandering soul, to the body. If the 'dead person' recovered, this was explained as the soul having wandered out into another world and now having been awakened and brought back. If not, the rites for mourning would begin. The practice of 'calling back the soul' varied according to the social status of the dead. For the royal or high official family, these rites were more complicated, and many more were needed, such as recalling the lost soul in the palace, in the capital and other places where the dead person used to be. 'Calling [the soul] back is the way in which love recovers its own consummation and has in it the mind which is expressed by prayer. The looking for it to return from the dark region is a way of seeking for it among the spiritual beings.' (Legge 1968: Vol. XXVII 167). Under Buddhist influence, this practice was, in some places, changed to the descendants of the dead shouting three times, facing west, in the hope of showing the dead the way to the western paradise, and praying their deceased parent or great-parent to become a *buddha* as soon as possible.

When a person died, he or she was believed to change his or her living place from the *yang* world to the *yin* world. For this change, there must be some permission from the *yin* world. A corresponding act which should be done immediately was to report the death to the proper governing authority in the underworld, through some intermediary such as Tu-ti (god of the land), Cheng-huang (god of the city), or Wu-tao (the god of the Five Roads), depending on local tradition, who would report further to the kings of hell. Only with their permission could the soul of the dead enter into the spirit world. In the social sense, relatives of the dead, especially when the dead was female, would be invited to discuss the mourning and burial details. It was extremely important to reach an agreement on the rites.

The mourning period from encoffining to burial varied from three days to three years. During this period, expressing the sorrowful feelings in suitable ways was expected. To express this kind of feeling publicly was the duty of the young to the old. 'The closer the kinship relationship, the greater is the expression of this sorrow'

(Hsu 1971: 159). The young should wear the mourning garments which were made of coarse white cloth or simply black clothes in modern times; the family members and close relatives were forbidden to attend celebration of marriage, festivals or any other joyful actions while they were in mourning. On the way to the graveyard, the direct descendants should hold sticks, which represent the 'root', to indicate that they would not forget where they came from; they should be wailing and should *kow-tow* before the coffin. The direct descendants of the dead person should also wear some kind of armband or headband, signalling the death of their parent, for a longer or shorter period.

Other rituals were to make sure that the spirit of the dead person could pass the journey from this world to that world and live a comfortable life there. These included dressing the corpse in his or her best garments, placing in the coffin gold, silver, pearls, or other objects of great value, and personal effects that the dead person was most attached to while living. There were additional practices such as scattering paper money at the head of the funeral procession, which was supposed to buy from the evil spirits the right to move along the road; burning clothing and paper money, which would be needed for the life in the other world; and, particularly in rich families, inviting Taoist or Buddhist priests to conduct religious services, every seventh day for forty-nine days, to aid the spirit in passing successfully through the necessary stages, such as the ten courts of judgement in the underworld, so that the spirit might not suffer severe punishment for the big or small wrongdoings committed while living.

Death marks an end of a life; however, this end is supposed to be only a change of the form of the family life. The Chinese not only believe that the dead is one of the links in the lineage, and has passed his or her contribution and duties to the next generations, but also hold that the ancestors still exist both in heaven and in the family. The only difference is that they had once been the living members and now they have become overseers of their descendants, and guardian spirits of the whole family enterprise. They are still to be treated as full members of the family and are provided with offerings, sacrifices, and reports periodically by the descendants. These offerings and reports are not only an expression of human emotion that refuses to let the deceased parents and ancestors simply disappear, but also a strong belief in the permanence of human life and human relationships. The value of an individual is revealed in the specially designed rites and is remembered in his or her contributions to the family. Therefore, though a person as an individual may pass away, he or she as a member of the family will live forever.

## FURTHER READING


Ahern, Emily M. (1973) *The Cult of the Dead in a Chinese Village*, Stanford, Stanford University Press.

Burkhardt, V.R. (1953) *Chinese Creeds and Customs*, Hong Kong, The South China Morning Post.

Doolittle, Justus (1865) *Social Life of the Chinese: with Some Account of their Religious, Governmental, Educational and Business Customs and Opinions*, vol. I, New York, Harper & Brothers.

Eberhard, Wolfram (1970) *Auspicious Marriage – A Statistical Study of a Chinese Custom* in *Studies in Chinese Folklore and Related Essays*, Bloomington, Indiana University Press.

Harrell, Stevan (1987) 'Domestic Observances: Chinese Practices', in M. Eliade (ed.) *Encyclopedia of Religion*, vol. 4, New York, Macmillan.

Hsu, Francis L.K. (1971) *Under the Ancestors' Shadow – Kinship, Personality, and Social Mobility in China*, Stanford, Stanford University Press.

Legge, James (trans) (1968) *The Li Ki*, in F. Max Müller (ed.) *The Sacred Books of The East*, vols XXVII and XXVIII, Delhi, Motilal Banarsidass.

Saso, Michael (1990) *Blue Dragon and White Tiger – Taoist Rites of Passage*, Washington, D.C., The Taoist Centre.

Wolf, Arthur P. (ed.) (1974) *Religion and Ritual in Chinese Society*, Stanford, Stanford University Press.

# 8. Japanese Religions

*Ian Reader*

## Introduction

The notion commonly expressed by Japanese people that they are 'born Shinto and die Buddhist' (Reader 1991: 7) is a clear and direct indication of the centrality of Japanese religious traditions to these major rites of passage and also of the interrelationship between different religious traditions in Japan. While degrees of conflict have always existed between the various religious traditions of Japan, these are less pronounced than the levels of mutual interrelationship and co-operation that exist, especially between Shinto and Buddhism, and that are most clearly expressed in the division of labour between these religions in dealing with the rites of passage of birth and death. In Japan, Buddhism is to a great extent a religion of death, and Shinto one of life, fertility, growth and production; hence while Buddhism deals with the rites of passage at the end of life, those rites and festivities that mark out stages in the development and celebration of life (e.g., birth and marriage) are more commonly found within the Shinto sphere.

Contemporary statistics produced by the Japanese Ministry of Culture show that some 115 million Japanese are classified as Shinto, and 92 million as Buddhist; along with the several millions affiliated to other religions. This makes a total almost double the population of Japan, and indicates that multiple belonging (usually of a Shinto–Buddhist nature) is common. This multiple belonging, along with Japanese affiliation to these religions in general, is based largely in the relationship between such major life-cycle events and the religious events that are called into play to deal with them. Many Japanese, for example, know little about Buddhism, even though their household is affiliated to a Buddhist temple. They may not even know what sect of Buddhism the temple belongs to until a family death occurs; the implicit assumption, however, is that a relationship exists between them and Buddhism, one that is especially concerned with the rites of death (Reader 1991: 3–4, 77–106). The relationship with Shinto is also acquired from social belonging: being born into a Japanese household, community and society confers a sense of belonging and of Japanese identity that is expressed through Shinto rites and customs.

The Japanese recognition that their very existence as social beings creates an involvement with their religious traditions is a dominant theme in Japanese religion, as is the social orientation and the social role played by Shinto and Buddhism. This recognition of the social nature of religion is further underlined by the various other rites and practices that occur at, and mark out, stages of the individual life-cycle. Rites marking the development of the child into a recognised social being, the official conferment of adulthood, marriage and the various times of life that are regarded as lucky or unlucky, have all at various times been recognised, dealt with and celebrated through religious rites of passage.

Some of these have, in modern times, disappeared due to the pressures and changing social and economic conditions of contemporary life which often do not allow for the long time demanded by initiation rites involving periods of seclusion and the like. Others, such as the ceremony conferring adulthood (*seininshiki*) at the age of 20, have become overtly secularised and are now carried out by civil authorities, in part at least because of the legal separation of religion and state that has come about since 1946.

Nonetheless all these, and other initiatory, rites will be examined below, as they emphasise the continuing importance of rites of passage and initiation in contemporary Japan, as well as the religious themes that remain implicit within them even when they may have become transposed into the civil sphere. None of these rites, even as they focus on the changes of status and position of particular individuals, is simply individual in nature. The following descriptions of life-stage rites and practices will show also their role in affirming social structures and in preserving and continuing the essential group relationships – especially the household and the local community – that frame the individual's position in Japan.

Before examining rites of passage in Japanese religious contexts two preliminary comments are necessary. The first is that historically there has been a strong tradition of regional variation in Japanese society and culture. Hence different regions have developed extremely disparate and differing practices; for example, burial customs and the rituals surrounding the disposal of the corpse, varied considerably from region to region. While contemporary developments have led to greater cohesion and to the consolidation of a more unified and homogenised culture, such varieties of regional custom still endure. Equally, while (for example) death rites are almost always Buddhist in nature,[1] one has to recognise that Japanese Buddhism has an extremely sectarian side to it, and that the rites as carried out in one sect are not necessarily followed in the same way in all others. In other words, rites may vary from place to place, and from sect to sect. Nonetheless, the underlying meanings within them tend to be coherent. The accounts that will be given here will describe the most common patterns and the basic underlying meanings that occur.

The second preliminary comment is that Japan is a highly modernised, economically advanced and urbanised society, whose population and economic focus have shifted during the past several decades from the agricultural and rural to the urban, industrial and, increasingly, the highly technological and financial, and from an extended family/household to a nuclear family structure. These changes have had obvious repercussions in religious terms: the social structures of religion predominant in rural, agricultural society have given way to the more individualised choices of urban life, and the processes of secularisation have made inroads into the former undifferentiated relationship between religion and everyday life. This has had an effect on rites of passage: customs and practices that were normal in earlier, rural Japanese society, and participated in by everyone, may no longer be relevant or practical in contemporary urban Japan. Rites of initiation into the local community, that played a prominent and vital function in small villages where everyone lived and worked in close proximity, often pooling their labour in rice growing and other communal economic activities, are less important, and may become marginal or irrelevant in urban communities where neighbours do not share the same economic livelihood, where they may go outside the local community area to work, and where their primary focus of allegiance and loyalty may have shifted from their neighbourhood to their work community.

Such changes have given the performance of passage rites, and rituals in general, a more voluntary nature than they used to have. Whereas village pressures and customs would mean that, for example, parents would feel obliged to observe the accepted procedures and rituals after a birth, the increasing individualism of modern Japanese urban society has allowed for greater degrees of choice as to whether one carries out some or any of the practices.

A further point of note is that the fragmentation of the traditional social structures of rural villages has weakened the main religions dealing with rites of passage, Shinto and Buddhism, both of whose strongest roots have been located in rural communities. Because, too, these religions have come to be identified more and more with social rituals, they have come to be seen, by large numbers of Japanese, as spiritually deficient and even moribund, little more than religions of social custom. Much of their religious dynamism, especially in terms of faith- and practice-oriented religious paths for the individual, has been taken over by the new religions, which represent the most powerful contemporary phenomenon in Japanese religion.[2] As this has happened, the religious constituents of Shinto and Buddhism have been gradually eroded, ironically making them (especially Buddhism with its connections to death and the ancestors) ever more increasingly dependent on their social position in dealing with rites of passage, which have come to occupy a central place in their contemporary teaching.[3]

## Individual life stages, rites and initiations

Life itself could be seen, in traditional Japanese folk belief, as constituting a series of stages marked out by rituals and religious ceremonies.[4] Many of the concepts underpinning these may still continue even as the rites that now occur have altered, become secularised or truncated. The birth of a baby occurs, according to folk belief, when a soul (*tama*) is given to it by the deity (*kami*) of birth. The thirty days afterwards were a period of seclusion, when both mother and baby were liminal and dangerous. Rites such as the naming ceremony, on the seventh evening after birth, when the baby was introduced to its relatives, served to help incorporate the new child into its family group and community, and to reintegrate it and its mother into the world. At the end of the thirty-day period the baby would be introduced to, and incorporated into, the wider world by being taken by its family, including the grandmothers, to a Shinto shrine (normally a local community shrine) to be blessed, introduced to the tutelary deity and placed under its protection.

The contemporary practice of giving birth in hospital has meant that mother and baby are scarcely separated from the wider world in the present day. However, some aspects and patterns seen in the earlier separation rites still linger. It is common for the mother to return to her parents' home, and to remain there for a month or so after the birth; hence she and the baby effectively undergo a rite of separation from their home community for a month or so. During this month-long period it is common for mother and baby to remain quietly indoors. The end of the seclusion comes with the return to the family home and the visit (*miyamairi*) to the shrine to have the baby blessed; the baby is wrapped in ceremonial garments, usually given by the mother's family. During the ceremony that follows the family prays to the deity, while the baby is encouraged to cry (to let the deity know it has a new parishioner!). Afterwards celebratory foods and *sake* are consumed. Often, too, afterwards, the baby will be introduced, before the family Buddhist altar (*butsudan*), to the ancestors who are enshrined there, and will be placed under their protection also.[5]

In contemporary urban Japan it has become increasingly common for parents to take their babies not to a local community shrine but to larger, more famous national shrines. This process, while confirming identity in and belonging to the wider community, also shows how identity values have shifted from the local and regional towards the national.

The next major age rite is *shichigosan* (the 7–5–3 festival) when boys of five and girls of three and seven are dressed in bright kimono (or, increasingly, in very smart western clothes) and taken, in mid-November, to the shrine to be given a further blessing. This rite was traditionally a recognition of the child's development and acquisition of a full social personality. Nowadays it is widely celebrated, as much as anything because it provides an opportunity for both parents and child to dress up, and to demonstrate their wealth and status. It is common for the parents to video the whole performance, and also for more time to be spent in dressing up and filming the child than in actually participating in the ritual events at the shrine.

Maturity and the conferment of marriageability were traditionally bestowed by rites which varied from region to region, but which generally removed an age-set of youths from their normal environment and made them take part in some religious performance involving either seclusion or ascetic practice. In the island of Shikoku, for instance, the initiatory rite that conferred adulthood and gave the person the right to get married, involved performing part of the 88-stage pilgrimage that circles the island. Normally youths would go in age-set groups to walk part of the route in early spring. Though the initiates would suffer some hardships in having to walk and sometimes to sleep out, it was also a festive occasion, for the route was full of groups of young people of both sexes who, while acquiring the status of maturity and marriageability, also had the chance to meet prospective mates. The initiates were clearly in a liminal state, having left behind their former settled status to enter a period when all normal patterns of behaviour were suspended while they formed a transient and ribald community with their age mates.[6] Such practices, which were common until the early decades of this century, virtually died out with the onset of war and the widespread call-up of rural youths into the army in the 1930s and 1940s, and with the food shortages that accrued as a result of these problems. After the war they never recovered. Many other age-set types of initiation, of which the pilgrimage example given above is but one variety, have gradually disappeared in the post-war period as economic pressures and altered work patterns, such as the move from agricultural work to factory and salaried work, have reduced the amount of time available to participants for ascetic practices and extended rites of seclusion.

In contemporary Japan the coming of age rite has become standardised and secularised, and any hint of religious austerity or of a period of liminality has disappeared. Nowadays, on 15 January each year a civil ceremony is held for young people who will become twenty during the year. After this they are legally considered to be adults and may marry without parental consent. The rite takes place at civic halls. Many, however, add a religious dimension by visiting, before or after, a Shinto shrine to pray for the blessing of the deity.

Other secular versions of initiation, which can be seen as rites of passage involving transformation of status and incorporation into new communities, are widespread in Japan. Schools, even nursery and junior schools for children of six or younger, have formal entrance ceremonies in which the children take an oath of loyalty and allegiance to the school and sing the school song. Such entrance rituals occur at every step up the educational ladder, even on entering university. Entering into regular employment is also an occasion for similar rituals. Company induction ceremonies generally take place in April (which is the start of the business and academic years), with all new employees formally incorporated into the company as a group in a mass ceremony. Such ceremonies are not, in the explicit sense, religious, as they do not occur at religious centres such as shrines or temples, and the officiants are not religious specialists but school or company officials. They do, however, express many implicitly religious themes, especially of a Confucian nature. The communal ritualism and swearing of oaths, the ideals of harmony and co-operation expressed through them, the affirmation of a hierarchic structure of relationships, with the new inductees swearing allegiance to those above them, and the creation of a sense of common identity in the participants through the shared ceremonies, are shot through with religious motifs that are designed to enhance the individual's sense of belonging and reaffirm the social order.

Besides these initiation and passage rites that mark out transitions, another commonly observed custom connected to age and to life stages is the widely held notion in Japan that certain ages are especially lucky or unlucky, and represent a passage into a new phase of life which may be (especially with unlucky ages) fraught with problems, and thus require some form of religious observance. Folk Japanese notions, absorbed largely from Taoism, of a sexagenary cycle saw the age of sixty-one (the start of a new cycle) as an especially fortuitous year, to be celebrated. Now that the attainment of advanced ages is commonplace, these lucky ages have ceased to be of major importance, but the unlucky ages (*yakudoshi*) of thirty-three for a woman and forty-two for a man continue to be regarded as rather problematic and transitional ages in which it is considered appropriate to visit a shrine or temple and place oneself under the protective benevolence of the deities or *buddha*s, and to receive a special purification to guard one in this transient phase. Some people also perform more extensive religious rites at this time, such as going on the Shikoku or another of Japan's major pilgrimages.

## Marriage

The use of religious rituals (most commonly Shinto, but occasionally Buddhist, and now quite often Christian) to celebrate weddings is comparatively recent; until the present century unions were inaugurated largely through social rites of gift exchange (Edwards 1989: 36–7). Because weddings are in fact, in the Japanese perspective, essentially a liaison between two households, their primary focus centres on rites involving the two households, and the movement of the bride (who traditionally leaves her home to enter her husband's household) from her own family into her husband's. These rites of separation and integration are surrounded by a process of exchanges of gifts and pledges of allegiance, and the ritual exchange of cups of *sake*. The rites usually occurred within the home, many of them before the family Buddhist altar enshrining the ancestors, to whom the new bride would be introduced as a new family member. In this century, however, largely as a result of assimilating western influences and customs, marriages have been taken outside the home to be celebrated at various religious centres. A religious ceremony, whether held at a Shinto shrine before the deities, at a Buddhist temple or at a Christian church, has now taken its place in this series of wedding rites, along with the exchange of *sake* cups, betrothal presents and the like. The date of its occurrence is generally determined after consultation with a diviner who will select an astrologically auspicious day on which the couple should unite. This custom remains widespread today.

Marriage has become a highly commercialised process, with the majority of weddings held in special wedding halls or hotels that cater almost exclusively for this purpose. Such centres can provide the facilities for Shinto and Christian ceremonies; some couples may even have both. The growing popularity of Christian weddings in the last decade or so has little to do with any growth in the Christian faith in Japan, and much to do with the fact that white weddings have come to be seen as extremely romantic. Indeed, many popular television dramas and films have revolved around white weddings, thereby enhancing their image. It has become fashionable also for couples to go on package holidays abroad that combine a wedding ceremony in a Christian church and a honeymoon in a suitably romantic setting. Current destinations for such tours include New Zealand, Australia, Europe (especially Paris) and Hawaii.

The overtly religious ceremonies that occur during the process of uniting the two households may often be a primarily decorative matter of ostentatious consumption and status-enhancing expenditure, while the essence of the meaning of marriage is centred in the rites and exchanges that take place between the two households to smooth the passage of the bride from her status as daughter in one household to wife and daughter-in-law in another.[7] The couples who go on package marriage tours abroad are likely also to have undergone these rites before departing.

## Death and beyond

By far the most important, widely observed and complex rites of passage in contemporary Japanese religious terms are those concerned with death. Their observance reflects the importance of concepts concerning the spirits of the dead and of the ancestors as continuing members and guardians of the household. Participation in the various rituals surrounding the dead, including *o-bon*, the Festival of the Dead, held in summer, remains the single most common religious action for the Japanese, close to ninety per cent of whom observe some or all of these rites either regularly or periodically.[8] While the basic ritual framework that envelops these rites is Buddhist, with rites performed at the home and temple by the Buddhist priest, many of the practices involved and many of the underlying notions are founded in the enduring Japanese folk religious tradition.[9]

The roots of these extensive rituals are found in Japanese concepts of death as a process of disruption, during which the soul (*tama*) leaves its home in the body to journey to the world of the dead and to become an ancestor. Ancestors are believed to remain in contact with the living of their household, and to guard and watch over them and succeeding generations. They also protect the fortunes of the household and act as symbols of continuity and tradition. If properly venerated they are benevolent but, like all Japanese spiritual entities, they have their potentially dangerous side as well and, if neglected, can cause misfortunes and afflictions to their living kin. Thus the relationship between ancestors and descendants, and between the living and the dead, is a reciprocal one. The living perform rites on behalf of the dead to lead them to full salvation and enlightenment in the world beyond, and the dead (ancestors) give protection and benefits to the living in this world.

From the early eighth century CE onwards Buddhism came to be the vehicle through which the rites surrounding death and the corpse, and the processes of veneration of the ancestors, came to be expressed. Over a period of centuries it gradually assimilated this role at all levels of the community until now death almost invariably is related to Buddhism in the minds of Japanese people.

During the period of separation from the body, the soul was traditionally believed to be dangerous and polluting and liable spiritually to harm or afflict those close to it in life, or even take its close kin with it to the netherworld. This liminally dangerous period, when the soul was still attached to this world, was considered to last for forty-nine days, during which time numerous rites took place to separate the soul from this world, purify it, and turn it into an ancestor. During this forty-nine day period the close kin were especially at risk from the predilections of the dead soul, and were themselves treated as liminal. They were in danger from the polluting effects of the spirit, and themselves carried the pollutions of death and so had to be separated off from their fellows. The period of forty-nine days' mourning is still quite widely observed, especially by the most immediate kin (e.g., husband or wife).

Despite the modernisation processes that have served to marginalise or truncate so many other religious ritual processes, those surrounding death have endured, as have many of the residual folkloric beliefs connected with it. Much of this is because the ancestors are venerated inside the household: their presence is marked by the *butsudan*, or family Buddhist altar inside the home, in which mortuary tablets denoting the ancestor are placed and venerated, often on a daily basis. Consequently, Japanese people grow up, from an early age, in the presence of the ancestors, and become used to paying homage to them as a household custom. Even where people may no longer cognitively believe in the presence of the ancestors as such, they may well venerate them as symbols of tradition and continuity.[10]

After death a bowl of rice is usually placed by the deceased's head to sustain the soul on its journey. A sword or similar tool, such as a razor, is also provided to help the soul protect itself against evil spirits seeking to lure it to the hells. A temporary altar with a photograph of the deceased is erected in the house, and neighbours and family come to pay homage. On the night before the funeral those close to the deceased stay up all night by the body, and the next day wash it and dress it in white (the colour in Japan of both purity and death). The clothes worn by the corpse in the coffin are tied or done up in reverse order to the way that they would be for the living. In some areas, such as Shikoku, the corpse is dressed in the traditional garb of a pilgrim, to indicate the journey that is about to take place.

Buddhist priests perform a series of rites (the numbers of priests and rites is dependent on the family's wishes and the amount of money it wants to spend) to provide the deceased with Buddhist teachings that will purify any sins and that will help the soul awaken to enlightenment and become emancipated and released from this world. After cremation, a small amount of ashes and bone is retrieved and placed in an urn which is then interred at the grave.

On the seventh day after death the dead soul receives a new name and identity to mark it off from this world and to give it a new identity in the next. This posthumous name (*kaimyo*) confers a Buddhist ordination and status on the deceased and symbolically extinguishes the material presence of the deceased. There is a distinct parallel here to the practice of giving the new baby its name and identity in this world seven days after birth; indeed, the whole series of rites after death and in the journey to ancestorhood in many ways mirrored, at least in earlier times, the various rites that occurred during the individual's lifetime. This name-giving also is similar to the Buddhist practice of giving a new name to Buddhist priests when they are ordained, thereby separating them from their old identities and giving them a new, religious persona.

The posthumous name is inscribed on two temporary, wooden mortuary tablets (*ihai*), one of which is placed in the *butsudan*, the other at the grave; the one at the grave gradually wears away, symbolising the physical disappearance of the body. At the end of forty-nine days the soul is considered to have become incorporated into the world of the ancestors, mourning ends and a permanent black lacquer *ihai* embossed in gold and engraved with the posthumous name is placed in the *butsudan*. It is to the *ihai* that prayers to and conversations with the ancestors are addressed, and to which offerings, such as bowls of rice, are made. Many people 'talk' to the ancestors, keeping them informed of family events, and giving them a sample of each meal, for the dead continue to be important members of the family. As was noted earlier, an important element in marriage rites is the introduction of the bride to her new ancestors at her husband's family altar.

Though the forty-ninth day serves as the end of the immediate series of rites of passage, the rituals connected with the dead continue for many years. The path to full salvation is linked also to the period of social remembrance, and generally speaking the dead person is memorialised for roughly the length of time that there are people alive who remember him or her as a social being. Periodic rites (on the hundredth day after death, the first, third, seventh, thirteenth, twenty-third and thirty-third anniversaries of death) continue the process. In addition, each year the ancestors are remembered at the *o-bon* festival in summer and at the spring and autumn equinoxes, when the family gathers to clean the grave and make offerings to the dead there.

These rites have endured remarkably well, especially considering how many other rites of passage in Japan have altered shape in recent times. While the form of some of the objects involved in the ritual process has changed in line with modern technological developments (for example special effects funerals and Buddhist altars with electronic doors and candles), the basic nature and format of the rituals, with the posthumous name after seven days, the Buddhist services, the period of mourning and the forty-nine-day period of rituals, have remained comparatively constant.

## Conclusion

The above description of rites of passage concerned with the life-cycle of individuals in Japanese religious contexts brings out some important points concerning the nature and incidence of rites of passage in general. The detailed and complex rites of passage of earlier ages, especially those focusing on the observance of taboos and of seclusions, whether to avoid pollutions, as with the mother and baby after birth, or in order to acquire new social status, have become simpler and shorter, often disappearing altogether. Many major times of rites of passage have become voluntary (e.g., the rites that may or may not follow birth), or have been taken over, albeit with implicitly religious motifs and formats, by secular authorities. At times overtly religious rituals appear to have been appropriated as adornments to familial ones, as with weddings. Only death continues to necessitate complex, continuing and religiously centred rites of passage; this is doubtless because of the highly developed practices of ancestor veneration and views of the spirits of the dead in Japan. However, as the cases above have shown, even if the length and intensity of many of these rites may have diminished, there remains a continuing religious dimension to many of them, while implicitly religious themes have permeated even the apparently secularised versions of passage rites into such institutions as schools and business organisations.

The Japanese case suggests that, as a society industrialises and modernises, and as it moves away from the close-knit environment of village communities into the looser frameworks of urban society, complex rites of passage, especially of an initiatory form, may become marginalised, losing their overtly religious dimensions and becoming voluntary rather than obligatory. However, the importance that continues to be placed on the rites concerning death and on the continuing relationship between life-cycle stages and religious traditions, along with the recognition that social situations are innately connected with religious belonging, show that the religious dimensions of rites of passage need not necessarily be marginalised in modern industrial societies. As the Japanese case demonstrates, they can continue to be an intrinsic part of the religious structure, confirming social, household and community identity; indeed, it would be reasonable to say that the vitality of both its main religious traditions, and especially of Buddhism, is intimately connected to the occurrence and continuation of such rites of passage. To a great extent, then, the Japanese continue to be 'born Shinto and die Buddhist', and to have their religious consciousness framed partially by the rites of passage these call into action.

## NOTES

1. It is not uncommon for Christians to 'die Buddhist'. Since Buddhism is the religion of the family/household, and since the bonds of the household are extremely important still, personal religious faith may well be sublimated to social custom and to the religious orientation of the household as a unit.
2. The literature on the new religions is extensive. For an introduction see

Reader (1991) pp. 194–233, and Helen Hardacre (1986) *Kurozumikyô and the New Religions of Japan*, Princeton, Princeton University Press.

3. I have discussed this question with regard to Buddhism in a number of articles: see Reader (1985) 'Transformations and changes in the teachings of the Soto Zen Buddhist Sect', *Japanese Religions*, vol. 14/1, pp. 28–48, and (1989) 'Images in Soto Zen: Buddhism as a religion of the family in contemporary Japan', *Scottish Journal of Religious Studies*, vol. 10/1, pp. 5–21.
4. A useful, if slightly dated, account of the series of rites that occurs within the life-cycle is that by Miyake (1972).
5. This abbreviated description of the rites surrounding birth is taken from Hendry (1981) pp. 200–5, which also describes several lesser rites that may take place in the first year or so of life.
6. The data on pilgrimage and initiation in Japan is based on Maeda Takashi (1971) *Junrei no shakaigaku*, Kyoto, Minerva Books, especially pp. 177–83, and Miyazaki Nishô (1985) *Henro – rekishi to kokoro*, Tokyo, Toki Shobô, especially pp. 194–5. The subject of pilgrimage and initiation, and of pilgrimage as a rite of passage is one that cannot, for reasons of space, be gone into here: it is, however, in Japan at least, a very important area in the study of rites of passage that deserves further attention.
7. I have touched only very superficially on the ritual processes involved in weddings. For fuller details see Hendry (1981), which concentrates on rural areas and more traditional weddings, and Edwards (1989) which looks at commercial weddings in special wedding halls.
8. These figures come from surveys conducted in Japan by various agencies including the *Yomiuri Shinbun*, one of Japan's major newspapers, and from discussions of Japanese practices and beliefs about the dead in the present day in Kômoto Mitsugu (1988) 'Gendai toshi no minzoku shinkô – kakyô saiken to chinkon', in Omura Eishô and Nishiyama Shigeru (eds) *Gendaijin no shûkyô*, Tokyo, Yuhikaku, pp. 33–76, especially pp. 43–7.
9. The most comprehensive account in English of Japanese practices concerning death and the ancestors is Smith (1974).
10. I have dealt at some length with these issues and with the relationships between ancestors, Buddhism and the household in Reader (1991) pp. 84–101.

## FURTHER READING

Edwards, W. (1989) *Modern Japan Through its Weddings*, Stanford, Stanford University Press.

Hendry, J. (1981) *Marriage in Changing Japan*, Rutland, VT, and Tokyo, Charles Tuttle.
Miyake, H. (1972) 'Folk Religion', in I. Hori, F. Ikado, T. Wakimoto and K. Yanagawa (eds) *Japanese Religions: A Survey by the Agency for Cultural Affairs*, Tokyo, Kodansha.
Reader, I. (1991) *Religion in Contemporary Japan*, Basingstoke, Macmillan.
Smith, R.J. (1974) *Ancestor Worship in Contemporary Japan*, Stanford, Stanford University Press.

# Index